BEAUTIFUL CHAOS

10 Questions, 20 Women, 200 Unfiltered Answers

BEAUTIFUL CHAOS

10 Questions, 20 Women, 200 Unfiltered Answers

MINDY JO NINO

Copyright © 2023 Mindy Jo Nino, All rights reserved.

No part of this publication may be reproduced, stored in a retrieval system or transmitted in any form or by any means, electronic, mechanical, photocopying, recording or otherwise, without prior permission of Halo Publishing International.

The views and opinions expressed in this book are those of the author and do not necessarily reflect the official policy or position of Halo Publishing International. Any content provided by our authors are of their opinion and are not intended to malign any religion, ethnic group, club, organization, company, individual or anyone or anything.

For permission requests, write to the publisher, addressed "Attention: Permissions Coordinator," at the address below.

Halo Publishing International
7550 WIH-10 #800, PMB 2069,
San Antonio, TX 78229

First Edition, June 2023
ISBN: 978-1-63765-408-8
Library of Congress Control Number: 2023909419

The information contained within this book is strictly for informational purposes. Unless otherwise indicated, all the names, characters, businesses, places, events and incidents in this book are either the product of the author's imagination or used in a fictitious manner. Any resemblance to actual persons, living or dead, or actual events is purely coincidental.

Halo Publishing International is a self-publishing company that publishes adult fiction and non-fiction, children's literature, self-help, spiritual, and faith-based books. We continually strive to help authors reach their publishing goals and provide many different services that help them do so. We do not publish books that are deemed to be politically, religiously, or socially disrespectful, or books that are sexually provocative, including erotica. Halo reserves the right to refuse publication of any manuscript if it is deemed not to be in line with our principles. Do you have a book idea you would like us to consider publishing? Please visit www.halopublishing.com for more information.

To the loves of my life:
Be safe. I love you.

Contents

Foreword	11
Introduction	13
Chapter One	27
Friendship: Acquaintance or Ride-or-Dier	
Chapter Two	49
Female Empowerment: What Does It Mean to You?	
Chapter Three	67
Dreams: Goals, Fantasy, or Reality	
Chapter Four	73
Career: How Has It Worked for You?	
Chapter Five	75
Relationship: Shag, Marry, Kill	
Chapter Six	95
Offspring: Pregame, Postpartum, or Hell No!	
Chapter Seven	117
Sex: The Forbidden Fruit or Let's Play!	
Chapter Eight	127
Shopping: Brand Whore or Red-Tag Diva	
Chapter Nine	136
Life Moment: The Day the World Stood Still	
Chapter Ten	144
What Do You Want the World to Know about You?	
Rachael's Beautiful Chaos	149
Ted's Beautiful Chaos	150

Juanita's Beautiful Chaos	153
Emily's Beautiful Chaos	154
Dolores's Beautiful Chaos	158
Mary's Beautiful Chaos	160
Malory's Beautiful Chaos	164
Stephanie's Beautiful Chaos	168
Ruth's Beautiful Chaos	170
Earth Angel's Beautiful Chaos	175
Veronica's Beautiful Chaos	180
Theresa's Beautiful Chaos	184
Porsha's Beautiful Chaos	188
Brooke's Beautiful Chaos	190
Zena's Beautiful Chaos	193
Dee Dee's Beautiful Chaos	196
Scarlett's Beautiful Chaos	198
Stacy's Beautiful Chaos	204
Jessie Wheaton's Beautiful Chaos	207
Camila's Beautiful Chaos	217
Concluding Our Chaos	231
Let's Connect	241

Foreword

I want to start by saying I am not a doctor, a nurse, a lawyer, a psychologist, or anything else requiring a degree or certificate. This book started as a passion project for a bored housewife who didn't know if or where she belonged, but then it took on a life of its own. I wondered if we women were all that different, or if there were more commonalities than we gave each other credit for.

As you move through this book, you'll see that I asked ten basic questions to nineteen women. Things that we do, talk about, or think of daily, but never put much effort into why. Why are we answering the way we do? How did we become who we are? Who shaped us? Are we happy? Would we change something—anything—if we could?

These were some of the everyday questions that were posed. With each answer, a silliness, a shyness, and sometimes a painful memory unfolded. Because of some of the details that will follow, I wanted to list a few national hotlines that can be used if you are in crisis. As you read on, you will learn that I stopped writing and interviewing women because of the pain it produced in me. My personal journey led me back to therapy, prayer, and many drunken nights.

We don't all respond or react the same, and some of us are further into the healing process than others. I attempted to be mindful of those still deep in their despair. Know that most of what you will read will be silly and upbeat, with cusswords peppered throughout, and some shady comments made by yours truly.

From the bottom of my heart, THANK YOU for spending your hard-earned money and for taking the time to read what's to come. I hope and pray that at the end of this, you feel more connected with me and with the other strange women who gave you a piece of themselves.

National Suicide Prevention Lifeline
1-800-273-8255

National Domestic Violence Hotline
1-800-799-7233

Substance Abuse and Mental Health Services Administration
1-800-662-4357

National Sexual Assault Hotline
1-800-656- 4673

Veterans' Crisis Line
1-800-273-8255 (Press 1)

LGBTQ National Hotline
1-888-843-4564

I understand that there are local and state hotlines and resources, but for obvious reasons, I won't list those. I really want you to fully enjoy and have fun with this book, but please, if you need to, utilize the above-referenced resources.

Introduction

Hey, beautiful!

Picture yourself with a cocktail in hand, mingling in a room full of people, and conversation is running rampant. Then the moment hits in which you are knee-deep in bullshit about how amazing Janet thinks her kid is at soccer at the tender age of three. With a lovely smile on your face, you nod in agreement as you quietly scoff while thinking, *Yes, lady, your kid is the next Cristiano Ronaldo, of course.* Or the woman next to you is holding her vodka neat with a twist of lime as she recounts how blissful her marriage has been for the last seven years. You know damn well that is a lie because if the vodka neat didn't give it away, the word "blissful" did. What about the woman who has dedicated her life to her career and next promotion?

I have run into a few of these women who have given me dirty looks or have been dismissive because I don't have a career. Hell, I don't even have a job.

School was never my thing. I barely made it out of high school, partly due to my horrific grades. The other factor was my unexcused absences that accumulated thanks to my skipping class all year. How'd I pull it off, you ask? I made up a few of the hours, as required, or submitted a couple of excuses forged with my parents' signatures. But, ultimately, the teachers and administrators could not tolerate me another year, so they passed me. In my defense, I was bored, not smart, because I had all the credits required to graduate my junior year, but my mother wasn't willing to allow me to graduate at the age of sixteen. It was probably for the best; my level of maturity failed miserably, as proven by my big mouth that got me kicked out of a health-career class during senior year. *C'est la vie.*

I dabbled in a few courses in varying community colleges and fared better. One of my favorite memories at one of the colleges was taking a history class, in which I made a friend. She happened to be the professor, told the silliest stories, and I failed her class. That's a whole other story.

I was never one to have a ton of friends, which led me to ask myself if I was emotionally and socially challenged to the point of being unable to make connections, or maybe I was simply a shitty person. My story is not pretty, and you will get to read about it as this all unfolds. With so many facets to my life, is this why I am skeptical about people and their stories? Is the three-year-old really that great at soccer? Is there a blissful marriage? Can you achieve great heights in life and still not be judgmental of what you may consider to be another's lack of success? Maybe? I hope so because the optimist in me desperately wants life to be full of rainbows and unicorns.

Being in a crowd gives me mixed emotions: happy, excited, nervous, anxious, pissy, annoyed, confused, etc. Sometimes I must excuse myself so my face doesn't give away what my mouth wants to say; when I do, it's usually too late. Oftentimes—actually, more frequently than I care to admit—I just say exactly what I think, to the detriment of all involved. My poor husband has his hands full with me. I often wonder if there is something wrong with him that makes him able to love someone so chaotic, or if he's preparing his path for sainthood. On the other hand, it takes one to know one. He's just as crazy, but in different ways.

I also wonder if my judgmental mind is overreacting, and whether I need to be more supportive. Is it normal to wonder if everyone is full of shit? Is it an asshole move to assume everyone is always hiding something? Or maybe my past experiences have jaded me into becoming a terribly judgmental person. I don't mean to be. I do enjoy hearing about people's kids, listening to those who have real-life love stories, and tales about women who didn't give up until they'd achieved what they wanted. No one's path is the same, regardless of where we end up. The cynic, the optimist, and the dreamer in me are often at odds with one another, and that makes for a nasty cocktail.

The other thought is that, perhaps, I am right. We all have insecurities or experiences that make us second-guess ourselves, others, and the world around us. Maybe there are others out there who will confirm I'm not alone in this way of thinking, or at least tell me I'm not totally wrong.

The wires that are crossed in my brain probably misfire more often than not, causing even more unnecessary electrical fires, which result in self-inflicted pain. Is that what is going on? That my brain overreacts and makes me the insufferable human I am? During the process of writing this book, I found that I wasn't alone—at least not completely.

Here's what you get for buying this book (other than making me one happy-ass bitch). You get to be a fly on the wall without any judgment. There is that word again—"*judgment.*" The ladies in this book and I are opening our hearts, souls, and mouths just for you. It's therapeutic to expel all those thoughts we have held on to for so long, regardless of how sane, vulgar, or erratic they are. This should be as if you were reading your best friend's diary, yet you have never met her. It's also to allow you a sigh of relief when the realization comes that you're not alone, that you can say out loud what you are feeling without suffering a harsh backlash.

I couldn't be more grateful for the women who participated in this shenanigan I call a book. Their willingness to be vulnerable to slake my desire to understand connecting to a stranger will forever be a priceless gift.

The most unexpected gift came at the end of the interviews when three things ultimately became clear:

> (1) With bad comes good; we just need to weather the storm. This idea was driven home after hearing the story of the buffalos. Simply put, they don't like water, and they sense when a storm is coming. They walk towards the storm, instead of running from it, thus cutting the time they must endure the storm and water. This will forever be something to remember. The bad times will come whether we want them to or not. So I will now choose to face the storm head-on and minimize my time of suffering.

> (2) The answers to each of these questions can and will change with every lesson learned, with each passing year, and with every tear and smile. Think of each movie or song that speaks of living each moment to the fullest or telling the people you love that you love them. With each laugh, we

gain a new perspective on a situation we may have just been crying about. It truly becomes a very personal journey…which leads me to number three.

(3) The same experience can manifest many points of view; it's our responsibility to respect each other nonetheless. What is heavy and difficult for one may seem senseless and miniscule to another. For instance, being raped was something that happened to me, but it wasn't violent. In my mind, I didn't ask for it or want it, but it was easier to just go with it because it would end faster. Although I don't think of it often, I would never tell another woman that she is overreacting. Same with money—I will pinch pennies and shop clearance for the rest of my life, regardless of my income, because I have a fear of not being able to provide for our kids. On the other hand, some may splurge because they have the confidence that it will all work out.

Each chapter dives into a seemingly basic question. For instance, in chapter two, we define empowerment as perceived through our own eyes. In chapter ten, I asked each woman to tell me what they desperately want the world to know about them. This question was particularly important to me as it's usually the one we carry silently. The one we answer while crying into our pillow in complete solitude. Do you know what the world knows about you? Is it an accurate depiction of who you truly are? Would you change the world's perception of you if you could? What would you do or say to ensure your legacy is what you want it to be?

I hope you enjoy getting the perspectives of all the women in one tidy yet foulmouthed book. It's not often you can get the unobstructed truth from so many people. Less than a handful of the women interviewed were from my inner circle or acquaintances; most of the interview subjects were women I had never met. I can't, for certain, give you statistics as to how many are married, gay, African America, Mexican, highly educated, or even clinically sane. What I can say is their answers just about blew my mind. Some of the answers were just one word, and that spoke volumes to me. The subject matter was either too much for them to unpack, or they just didn't want me to know about their vulnerable history—especially if they were one of my personal acquaintances—and that's okay too.

Others went into great depths. I spent an average of two hours per interview; there were laughs, lots of tears, and thoughtful probing into their responses to ensure accurate representation. These women not only inspired me to be more open and understanding, but to seek professional help for my past traumas. There were times I stopped writing or interviewing because it was too painful for me to continue. I became connected to these strangers in a way that allowed me to develop feelings I thought I had long healed from, but really had just shoved deep down.

At the time of this entry, I have been working on this book for about five years. That's right—five years. I took time with each person, each entry, each word, trying to make it perfect. One of the greatest lessons I learned is that there is no such thing as perfection. I think we all know this, but our deeper feelings and trust in this statement are sketchy at best. Once I felt a wholehearted connection with that concept, it helped me become more comfortable with my story and with this project. Do not get me wrong; if Yoda made a summary judgment of me, it would be, "The bullshit is strong with this one." I say this because I still have those days in which I bullshit my way through the darkness. Fake faith is better than no faith, in my opinion, because I refuse to submit to the most fucked-up version of myself.

What I want you to keep in mind is that these marvelous women are just who they are. I am not changing their wording, influencing their answers, or leaving out a response that doesn't meet my perspective eye to eye. Some women were very pointed and others…not so much. The women in the not-so-much crowd were the hardest interviews to get through. Also keep in mind they neither had nor will have any financial gain from this process; it was strictly done selflessly and voluntarily.

Set your mind at ease knowing that my deep, dark secrets are in this book too. It was a challenge to disclose the shit show I call life because it would be easy to figure out who I'm speaking of by giving the details. I would hate to publicize someone else's life just because their paths crossed mine; they didn't sign up for this. Keeping their names out of the book was the best way I knew to be honest with you and not hurt or screw someone over in the meantime. I did, however, get permission from my husband and each of my kids to tell my story, of which they are a huge part. They have been unwaveringly supportive in a way I had never known, and they believed in me in a way I could not have imagined. I'm beyond thankful and blessed for the five people I love the most in this world! They fucking rock (even when I cuss them out)!

Anyhow, I could bore you with society's statistical categories of who I am, but I won't, at least not now. Instead, what I really want to say is that I am an organized person, a superb hostess, the president of the PTA, and a snack-bearing football mom who kisses away boo-boos, all while being a sublime mix of Princess Kate and a sexy porn star as a wife. It would bring my heart joy to say I've never fucked someone over or been that dreadful villain in someone's story. I'd like to say that my confidence is strong, I have answers to most questions, and I've checked off many things on my bucket list. I could also lie and say I have never been embarrassed of my past behavior.

Let me start off by telling you that I have lost track of the bullshit and a half about which I am embarrassed. My mistakes and stupidities have made some people cry or laugh, and others (perhaps the smart ones) just walked away. The crazy thing is that it is not always alcohol induced. Sometimes I just say and do stupid shit. Maybe my mother was right; I'm the "Louie" of the world. This is what she has always called me. Her "Louie" was essentially the failure and disappointment of the family. The bar was set fairly low for me, and there were times I failed to reach even that height.

Now back to the Rubik's Cube that is my life. I do not have a bucket list, and everything I think I would put on one kind of scares me. Turns out that I'm forgetful. Like losing three debit cards in six weeks, or not finding my car keys for three months, only to find them in the key box (where they belong). I am often winging daily life like a bad eyeliner tutorial. Most days my biggest accomplishment is not having to call 911. I feel I'm some cross between Karen Walker from *Will and Grace*, Monica from *Friends*, and Charlotte from *Sex and the City*. It's exhausting being me.

I have four kids, three dogs, and a husband. I promise that I know their names, but usually not when I'm yelling at them. *GASP* Did I just say that I yell at my kids?! I sure as hell do! Guess what? I also yell at the dogs…and the husband…and anyone during a heated conversation after I've had a glass of wine. Oh, who am I kidding? I drink the whole bottle because no one likes a quitter!

So now that you have a warm and fuzzy feeling about me, here are the life facts you'll find in my obituary: I am a loving mother to four wonderful kids, a devoted wife to an ex-military man, a daddy's girl, a big sister to a little brother, Kelley's bestie, a friend to awesome people, and an asshole to some. Do you think an obituary would allow the word "asshole"? I love deeply and fight passionately, as I am an emotionally driven person. I love being around people and sitting alone in silence just the same. Truth be told, I need that balance. You will never hear someone saying, "Oh, Mindy Jo? Yeah! She had it all figured out." In reality, I'm a complete wreck who refuses to give up. There are moments that feel as if I couldn't ask for more and things are the epitome of perfection. Other days, I struggle to get out of bed, much less shower, because life hurts.

My personality goes from being quiet, observant, and nervous…to being the loudest in the room, the crazed dancing queen, and having zero inhibitions. The hardest moments come the day after my outgoing self makes her presence known. The feelings of guilt and shame are strong. I'm still learning to live with being okay with that part of myself since that's the part most people try to silence. Consistently being told that your wild spirit needs to be tamed can—and in my experience, does—become disastrous for your soul.

Being a mom has been the most amazing blessing, even on the days that I wish the firehouse would take teenagers and not judge me. My husband and I have been married for about eighteen years. We have experienced every emotion imaginable throughout that time. I can honestly say that I love him more today than the day we married, simply because life has happened, and we didn't give up on each other. On the other hand, for the same reason, I hate him more today than the day we married. You totally get that, don't you? My life, like everyone else's, has been a rose garden. It has been beautiful, lovely, and colorful. But, as in all rose gardens, it has its thorns. Those times that have been so painful, hurtful, and scary. Can't our thorns be admired just as much as our petals? I think God has also manicured my garden with life's manure to fertilize my ability to grow. Thankfully, I'm not who I was twenty years ago. We all need the shit to appreciate the beauty we have been given—some of us more than others. Let me be honest; I probably created my own messes seventy-five percent of the time. And yet, here I go, walking through my garden while admiring the view.

When I began this journey, I wanted to give the women the option of using their real names. However, after much consideration, names have been changed to protect the identity and privacy of our participants. Some of them talk about the real struggles of motherhood, infidelity, death, rape, and sex. It was important to me to respect their privacy, as some of the topics can be invasive, personal, and leave you feeling vulnerable when questions are answered honestly and wholeheartedly. It didn't feel right to expose anyone for my personal gain.

On the other hand, some of the women are nasty freaks, seven days a week, and don't want their lives chatted about at the next soccer practice. I'm only (kind of) kidding. Sex can be a huge part of life for a lot of reasons, and not everyone is okay with letting those skeletons run amok as if they were a bunch of six-year-olds on sugar highs at a Halloween festival. Regardless of the reason, I didn't use anyone's real name. They are all fabricated names the women chose or I assigned at random. I wanted to use the names on Bravo's *Real Housewives* because I'm just a little obsessed with this modern-day phenomenon that we call reality, but I didn't want any legal issues. Ugh, and don't even get me started on my fixation with Andy Cohen. Where's a heart emoji when you need one?

The only way this book was going to be what I wanted was for it to be as real as I could make it. We often live life walking a straight line, our voices muffled or simply silenced. Not this time. Not now. Not when we have so much to say.

Along with a name, some of the ladies have given me a tagline. Who doesn't love a good tagline? This is, again, all about anything they wanted. These taglines have been a hoot! What's mine you ask? "Fuck it, it can't get any worse." This plays over and over in my head. I say it out loud, hoping it will subconsciously make me feel better. In reality, I worry about everything from bills to my own reflection. If you have a tagline or motto, do you believe in it? Has it changed over the years with you? Since we're on the subject, if you don't have one, what would it be? Would your tagline be funny, serious, spiritual, or goal oriented?

Sidenote: Please don't go trolling my social media pages, fulfilling your personal curiosity and looking for a picture to connect to the women in this book. Most of them are not my Facebook friends or followers, and even if they were, I would never tell.

Let's have some unscripted fun and meet some of the ladies who have submitted a tagline!

Elizabeth: "I'm kind of a big deal!"

Ted: "To love is to educate, and to educate is to love."

Dee: "I will destroy you in the most beautiful way possible, and when I leave, you will finally understand why storms are named after people," and, "You can't come to my party! You aren't a VIP."

Kay: "A woman gives so much of herself to her husband, children, friends, and family, and no one ever checks to see if she's REALLY okay."

Theresa: *"En la vida, todo se save*...sooner or later, everything comes to light."

Malory: "It is what is." But my favorite quote is, "There's nothing in life to fear other than fear itself," by Franklin Delano Roosevelt.

Brittany: "I'm not lost; I just take the scenic route."

Veronica: "I have no clue...like, no clue at all."

Jessie Wheaton: "We would all be better off losing our damn minds. I'm just one of the crazy ones who knows it."

Camilia: "No one else really knows what the fuck they are doing, so do whatever the fuck YOU want to do."

After reading this book, I hope that you will have come to the realization that we can all connect with a complete stranger. Our lives don't have to be parallel for us to bond; just one intersection can have a monumental impact as we navigate our existence. Often we are so focused on making ourselves and others fit neatly in a box that we forget to celebrate our differences. We lose that basic human need to feel connected because we have whatever reservations that are blocking our possibilities. In my case, the biggest obstacle for me to overcome has been my personal insecurities, which cause me to be judgmental.

What is your roadblock? In this day and age, would it be political? Would it be fear of change, or fear of *not* changing? Are you still running from your past? Is your self-worth challenging you and keeping you from seeing or living your full potential?

As stated, I'm guilty of doing just this: being a judgmental bitch. I often meet someone and think, *How in the world will we be able to connect? They don't have kids; I have four. They aren't married; I've been married for a minute. They are well traveled and educated; I've seen Texas and Tennessee, and barely graduated high school. They exercise and eat healthily; I love to drink wine, eat tacos—I'm a gordita.* This was the whole basis for why I started to look past the bullshit and realized how much these people enriched my life. They brought so many perspectives that helped me grow as a mother, as a wife, and ultimately as a person. It's to you strangers and acquaintances who have propelled me into the possibilities of intersections that I say, "Thank you!"

As you read along, you will notice that the answers to each question vary in so many ways. Each woman was given her own chapter in which to celebrate her marvelous life. Their answers are as unique as the individual who answered them, yet we can see ourselves in their place as well. I couldn't help but be moved by some of their answers, and I laughed my ass off at others. There are one-word answers, and others that are lengthy. It is what it is. Being unscripted is a beauty in and of itself. Loving that raw person inside of us whom we often hide is liberating, and I hope to fully embrace myself one day.

Grab some wine, a hot cup of tea, or a pint of ice cream, and enjoy.

WARNING: I will not be held responsible for the caloric or alcoholic intake while indulging in these lives. Laughing until you cry or pee your pants is allowed. If you are my age or older, then you know what I mean.

Happy reading, lovies!

Chapter One
Friendship: Acquaintance or Ride-or-Dier

Grab a cocktail because we're spilling the tea on our besties, those bitches, and ourselves!

Acquaintances

At some point, I read on a social media post that someone didn't have time for or want "part-time people" in their lives. For a quick minute, it made me feel something, but I couldn't pinpoint what. After thinking about it for a while, I realized it just made me sad. I've seen this person's posts and comments several times; there's always a mix—a godly scripture, some rant, a praise of the day, or a "Why me?" This person shares pictures of themselves, their kids, sports, etc. I really enjoy it.

We met in passing at work and I thought this person was cool; friendly, somewhat outgoing, and witty. I have a lot of people on social media whom I follow even though they are "part-time people," commonly known as acquaintances. In fact, this person and I are acquaintances. We are part-time people who are in each other's lives by following each other via social media; we have a few commonalities, and respond to each other's posts every so often. I happen to like it this way. I am happy being a part-time person.

Could you imagine getting to know each person's kid(s), partner, parents, or their friends? How long would that take? Quite frankly, I don't know that any of us could truly give ourselves one hundred percent to everyone. What about the people who were meant to be in your life for only a brief moment to learn a particular life lesson, versus those who are in your life forever to help you with the sack of bricks we all carry? Do you believe in this in-the-moment versus long-term idea? Part-time people—a.k.a. acquaintances—are almost as important to me as my lifelong people.

Now, in this instance, I do not think this person was particularly talking about acquaintances. I believe they were talking about those people who say they'll be there no matter what and then ghost you at the slightest inconvenience. You're there, calling in the calvary as you wave your proverbial white flag, and they are back in town slamming pints at the local pub. Then you hold their feet to the fire by confronting them on their failed attempt at being a friend, and somehow it becomes your fault. I've had more than my share of these people in my life.

The other people I have a major issue with are those who don't know you exist the moment you leave the room. The truth is that life moves on, and we just lose touch. However, my self-absorbed, petty, and rather frail ego leads me to believe that I just didn't mean anything to the person who seems to have forgotten I exist. After years of therapy, I know that it's an "abandonment issue," as my therapist calls it while writing only God knows what on her legal pad to use against me at a later time.

I have been on both sides of being a part-time person. I'm sure we all have. It may not be one of our proudest moments, but it gives us something on which to reflect and learn. Here are two of my personal stories of being on either side of the part-time fence.

Let's start with the shitty me, the me who is flawed, heartless, and selfish. I met this woman through our kids who went to school together, and, come to find out, her family lived just a few blocks from us. The kids occasionally came over to our house to play, as most elementary-aged kids do. They were supersweet and respectful. The little girl had an infectious smile, and the little boy was as rambunctious as my third child. As much as the kids got into, they never got into something out of the ordinary. It was the classic tale of childhood friends running around a neighborhood and having fun.

When I met their mother, she stopped by while out for a walk with her youngest kiddo and introduced herself. We really hit it off. She was down-to-earth and had a knack for making me laugh at everything she said. She had this honesty that I have found in a lot of Latin women; you think they are kidding, but, really, they are telling you straightforwardly where they stand—if you don't like it, go fuck yourself—with smiles on their faces. I like it, but it's a trait I have never learned. I smile at someone, and they think I've stolen something from them.

Either way, we started spending more time together, and her youngest became my husband's favorite kid. After about six months or so, something devastating happened in her world. She was absolutely crushed and blindsided—you know, just going through the motions. This is where things started to change.

I did my best to be supportive and understanding. I tried to comfort her when she cried, give her the support I thought she needed—or at least the support I knew how to give—and be there to take the kids to help ease the situation.

My point of view was obviously skewed. I wasn't the one going through this; I was wrapped up in my own shit. At that point in my life, hindsight being what it is, I wasn't capable of being a good friend to anyone. I tried, but it wasn't enough. Fast forward maybe six months and she had become comfortable with what I offered and with her situation. She began opening up about the ongoings of her life to others around her, which gave her a much larger support system.

Things got to a point that she would tell her story to anyone who would stand still for five minutes. I kid you not; she would literally tell her story after meeting someone twenty minutes prior. It was similar to passing out hors d'oeuvres with a side of sour conversation. Not what I would do (I would have waited until we were all drunk), but you do you, boo face.

Anyhow, I grew tired of her showing up for me to make dinner for her and her kids. I was tired of always being the one supporting her through her issues because she was never able to reciprocate and be there for me. Logically I knew she was devastated by what was going on in her life, and she desperately needed a strong support system. My own craziness and selfishness made it difficult for me to be that long-term support. I wanted to; I thought I could be, but I ultimately failed. I became frustrated, and the relationship started feeling heavy.

Here's where I made a wrong turn and became the Wicked Bitch of Tennessee. I confided in one of our mutual friends (we'll call her Friend B) about how I was feeling. I told her that I was tired of the same song and dance that had taken over our friend for a year by then. I said I felt horrible for what she was going through, but I couldn't keep up anymore. I told her that I missed who she was when I first met her. And I said I was over listening to the same story a thousand times over. As the story goes, I eventually pissed off this Friend B by saying or doing I don't know what one night that I was trashed beyond belief. Being trashed isn't an excuse for being a shitbag, but (at the time) I would love to know what actually happened; I obsessed over it for months. A few years ago, though, I stopped giving a rip about what I might have done. Fuck that bitch.

Long story short, Friend B went and told Friend A everything I said, but I guess put her own negative spin on it. I have no idea what was actually said between them, but by the way things ended, I'm sure it wasn't pleasant.

When it all came down, Friend A did the right thing and confronted me face-to-face without raising her voice even once. It was a side of her I had never seen, calmness and candor. I had only ever seen the ten on the one-to-ten spicy scale of her fire. She asked me what happened that fateful night, but I couldn't remember. I knew what I had said prior to that night months before and confessed my sins as if sitting nervously in a dark confessional room with my priest the week before my First Communion.

She didn't forgive me. She told me I had lost her trust and things would never be the same. It really sucked. She had every right to be disappointed, angry, and hurt by me.

Towards the end of that friendship, I had the pleasure of witnessing that she had pulled through the darkness and found so much light for herself. When I met her, I knew her laugh was sincere and wholehearted. She'd lost it during her trial, as we all do, but it was coming back in full force. This time, it was that bottom-of-the-barrel type of strength and light. At the beginning of that awful drunken night, I was asked how Friend A was doing, and I told Friend B just that. How things went so wrong, I'll never know.

What I do know is I should have said no to Friend A. I knew she was weak and going through so much, but I failed by not telling *her* directly how I was feeling and by not setting healthy boundaries. Instead, I told Friend B what I was feeling, and as it turns out, she twisted the way I vocalized my frustration, making it look as if I were just talking shit. I don't blame Friend A for being pissed at me. She had every right to feel betrayed and backstabbed.

Ultimately, what I learned was, regardless of how we feel or perceive something, knowing you hurt someone you care about is the most important issue at the time. The other thing I learned is that honesty is the key. See, someone may not like what you have to say, but at the very least, they will have your honesty. Let me say it again for the cheap seats: I failed Friend A.

The end of this friendship stings the most out of all the lost friendships because the kids were all great friends. Prior to the event that set this in motion, they played together every day, spent the night at each other's homes, and went to school together. I later found out that her kids stopped speaking to my kids because of what I did. That was a travesty. You know, I'm not in any way holding ill feelings towards Friend A or her children because they defended their mother, and I was in fact the villain. My lack of vocalization and honesty ruined several friendships.

I did send a text after some time to let her know how sorry I was, but it was too late. That costly lesson hurt five people. It will forever be the one I regret the most. I will forever think of her and her kids. I will forever remind myself of that costly lesson and hope she is getting the best that life has to offer. I will forever hope and pray her kids are happy and healthy. I'm also deeply sorry to my own children for ruining what they had.

On the other hand, another friendship stands out because I poured my heart and soul into it, thinking she was a lifelong friend. Are you thinking what I'm thinking? Yes, karma's a bitch, and the bitch came knocking. Anyhow, it was great so long as there were parties to be thrown, barbecues to be had, alcohol to be consumed, or something was going wrong in my life. Our families got together for Sunday dinners. We used to go over to each other's homes in pajamas just to have coffee. We threw birthday parties for each other and our kids. No, let me correct that statement; she threw parties for her family and herself at my house. I didn't mind because we weren't drinking and driving, and our kids were safe. My husband and I would drop everything when they called if they needed something. Did this not mean anything?

It was when we really needed them that they were nowhere to be found. Ever. Well, maybe not ever. On the rare occasion they would help, that assistance always came with some sort of backhanded comment.

I noticed how wrong things were when others came around; the dynamic changed considerably. I finally gained enough courage to speak up and was greeted with excuses. I kind of just wanted them to listen. I just wanted them to acknowledge that not only did they let me down, but also they let down my husband and kids. The whole "we're family" really took a turn. After time ran on, we were able to move forward in a positive direction—or so I thought. The dynamic eventually changed so considerably that there is no longer a relationship, but I loved and learned. Now, when I think of them, I feel a slight sting. I'm sure, if asked, she could come up with a thousand reasons why things ended the way they did.

Remember when I said I was a shit show? I was a shit show with her as well. I trusted her, so I let go of inhibitions to give her my truest self, to share some of my darkest moments with her. In the end, I was a lot to handle when I drank with her. It was usually in good fun, but Patrón and I were in a love-hate relationship. Every time he and I took a spin, I danced like a crazy person, got naked, or fought. Now, he and I have sporadic rendezvous, but we have agreed to be nonexclusive and entertain each other no more than once a year.

Looking back on my time with this lady, one of my favorite memories with her was completely unexpected. I had gone to her house on my way to T.J.Maxx to see if she wanted to go buy a gift with me (just one of the fun things we used to do). Anyhow, she had a couple of shots of moonshine and nothing else to do. We started with one shot, which led to a beer, then to more shots. We never made it to T.J.Maxx, and I was DONE! As we sat drinking, laughing, and listening to music, we thought it would be a good idea to post a "checked in" at a local bar just to mess with her husband. We couldn't stop laughing when he called to bitch us out. He quickly learned we were messing around and laughed with us. After a while, she took a picture of me passed out on her patio table and posted it on Facebook. She was notorious at posting pictures or videos of anyone in compromising situations. Something I never liked, and it made me extremely uncomfortable.

Her demand for outer perfection was her biggest downfall, in my opinion, because as I learned, she was willing to throw anyone under the bus for her own sake. Long story short, we laughed so much that day, as we did most of the time we spent together. It was those days and moments that kept me going back for more—it was intoxicating to laugh that much.

I don't regret any moment I spent with her. You see, I knew her downfalls and weaknesses, but I loved her. I accepted her as she was because who the fuck is perfect? I know I'm not. I've been told about sketchy things I've done while drunk, and I can't say they've been my proudest moments. Hell, I've had many sober moments that make my stomach turn.

I don't know if the drinking was the part that bothered her as much as when I would just call her on her shit. If I know anything, it's how wrong I can be. She, on the other hand, had this superiority complex with me. It was like a light bulb came on one day when I realized that she wasn't just talking shit about others to me; she was talking shit about me to others. The difference was that I was too stupid to keep my mouth shut when I felt that betrayal. That didn't go well, to say the least. I told a few people what she had been saying, they confronted her, she covered for herself, they believed her, and I was out. Did I learn my lesson to keep my mouth shut? Nope. However, I have *hopefully* learned to say what I need in a productive, honest way. There's a difference between how I've communicated in the past and how I try to convey my thoughts now.

Just so you know, we still chat every now and then. The random texts and videos bring so much to my day. I'm thankful to have had her in my life the way I did, even if things changed. What I imagine won't change is the way we make each other laugh. If there is anyone I can get into trouble and have a blast doing it with, she would be the one—so it's probably best that we now live fourteen hours apart.

The caveat to my ups and downs in any situation is that it takes so much for me to move forward. I feel pain, and I truly have to process through all the muck in my head. That's a lot of shit. My husband gets tired of my talking about things because it's as if we're on a toxic merry-go-round that is the only ride still partially functioning in a broken-down, deserted carnival I call my brain. This ride doesn't have a catchy name, but if it did, it should be something that induces night terrors. What it does have is the who, what, where, when, and how. It leaves me with that sick feeling and the need to purge my heart, mind, and behavior. I go round and round with what I did wrong. Where was the left turn? Who is at fault? Is anyone at fault? How could I have been better? Did I apologize correctly? Do I even understand why this happened? How do I learn? What is the real lesson? Y'all, it's a whole thing, and it's exhausting!

Either way, when I finally move forward, we're done. I owe you nothing, you owe me nothing, and don't expect a damn thing from me ever again. HA! Those are lies I tell myself to feel strong. In all actuality, most of the people who have left my life can call me, and I would answer. I may not go the extra mile or trust them ever again, but I'm a sucker for not wanting to see anyone hurt or in pain. Let's face it, I have boundaries that would make most therapists cringe. The good news is that not all my relationships are this bad.

At the time of writing this entry, I have just over 500 Facebook friends. I promise there is no way I'm in a ride-or-die relationship with each of them. As a matter of fact, I'd like to multiply my following on social media in hopes someone thinks I'm writing a book worth reading. Prior to this, I loved getting an insight into the thoughts and opinions of others. What can I say? I'm nosy. You can tell a lot about a person by what they post. Everything from political views, religion, what types of nightclubs they prefer, or the kind of parent they are. It's fascinating to scroll through any social media outlet and see what is going on in the world that day—near or far. Imagine it as if it were people-watching at Walmart. I know I will never know the truth about how they live, but would I ever want to? Honestly, no. I found that when interviewing women for this book, it was much easier getting raw answers from strangers whom I would never see or speak to again than from women I actually know.

The funny part is, when you have some insight into a person's life, you can see, more often than not, that what they post on social media is vastly different from their real lives. But we all know that happens, right? Like, hot damn she looks better than a Victoria's Secret model on vacation! Then you run into them at the grocery store and see them without the filters and angled lenses; all of a sudden, they've shrunk eight inches and gained sixty pounds since last week! Well, duh, I'm totally guilty of doing the same thing. You know what a filter or lens can't fix? A relationship status.

I will grace these people with the title of Romantic Pioneers. Visions of knights in full armor, off on their next quest to find love, fill my imagination. Can you see it now? You know, the ones who have a new partner every six months, deeply and passionately in love by the end of the week, yet it ends in flames like a good hibachi grill? No judgment at all.

Knowing that someone can be that reluctant to give in is fascinating. Your ability to endure the trials of your search is admirable. It's more probable that it's toxic, but I'll still applaud your tenacity.

You know which ones I keep the farthest away from and will never be friends with? Family members. At least most of them. Yeah, if anything good came from me leaving Texas, it was the separation from it all. I cannot stand to see the cheerful salutations on social media, full of pretty emojis, and then see the same family members at Grandma's house that weekend, and all they do is talk shit behind each other's backs. Or when the women in your family make light of, or make excuses for, the disgusting maggots in the male population, which includes their sons and spouses. I would use gasoline to put them out if they were on fire. Who am I kidding? Gas prices are on the rise, and I'm broke as fuck. Let 'em burn, and we'll call it the pregame before they burn in hell.

Oh, and those that yak, yak, yak at the top of their lungs, thinking it will get them somewhere, yet they have zero clue what they are talking about! All I want to say to them is, "For fuck's sake, shut up!" But no matter how loud I said it, they'd never hear, never understand.

We live only an hour away from my family, and I can count on one hand how many times I've gone to see them in the last four years. I tried when we first moved back to Texas, but then I realized nothing had changed in fourteen years. The only downside to staying away is how much I miss my grandmother; I cannot see her alone because there's always someone around. The upside is how private I prefer my daily life. None of them need to know about me or my family. The irony of that statement doesn't fall on deaf ears.

Now, there are those cousins whom I do see and with whom I make a point of staying in touch (via social media), but I can't say we are as thick as thieves. They are the ones who stay out of the drama and keep to themselves. From what I've learned, they are the smarter ones. A trait they have in common—and that I admire—is that they are fully capable of disagreeing and being honest with each other without being offended. Then again, maybe I'm blinding myself to who they really are because that's what I would like to believe. It's refreshing to focus on the good in my extended family since I hear that cousin best friends are a different breed—and I'm happy for those who are.

With all that said, I would define friendship as multidimensional, or like a bull's-eye; the closer to the center, the more critical you are. A bull's-eye reference is obvious and basic, right? But a multifaceted jewel can make any woman happy. Stay with me; you have the integral point of the jewel, but every point and facet makes it shine with distinctive brilliance. In an exceptional way, each person in your life makes you unique, individual, and bright. As individuals, we have so many sides to ourselves. It's not a bad thing, and please do not confuse it with being two-faced.

For instance, one person may feed my spirituality while another feeds my crazy. How can you have a group of girlfriends and each not bring a different strength? I'm not always sure of what I bring to the table, but I hope honesty is at the top of the list. I think it's when you can't be honest or comfortable with yourself about who you are that you feel two-faced or hypocritical—I'm guilty of both on some level. For instance, your past has been filled with sexual endeavors; then you marry money and all of a sudden get righteous with others at the mention of a penis. The other type of people I roll my eyes at are the ones who talk shit about being loyal, but are the first to stab you in the back.

Therefore, I'm mostly an acquaintance. I have a hard time making friends just because I get into my own head, and at times, I'm introverted. I enjoy being around people, laughing at nothing, and keeping things simple. However, I undoubtedly hate getting home from work (when I do hold down a job) to four kids and finding someone at my door, waiting for and expecting me to tend to them as well. I have had this happen to me a couple of times. Those friendships didn't end well either.

I cannot deal with my shit then baby you because you don't want to deal with yours. This may sound familiar from the previous description of my failed friendship, but what I'm speaking of now is how it becomes problematic when done day after day. Oh, and heaven forbid I tell you the truth about how I feel when you do these things to me; then you're offended. I want to shake the shit out of people like that! Grow the fuck up. Understand I ain't your mama or your dude, so I have no reason to coddle you.

I probably don't understand what these types of people want or need, as I have a hard time figuring myself out. I'm the type who steps up to help at the drop of a hat, but will do everything by myself without asking for help. When I offer to help you, it's because I don't mind. But do not *demand* anything from me.

I have a handful of friends who can totally count on me at any time of the day or night, and they would never abuse it. I think that's the difference. They just get it. They get me. They would truly take care of my family and me the way I do for them.

The others whom I have experienced expecting things from me seem to be those I wouldn't trust to care for my dog, much less my children. This may come across as, "I'll only do for you what you do for me," but it's not. Every selfless asshole has a breaking point. Why? Because I'm not Mother Teresa, and the option of my being nominated for sainthood was revoked at the age of ten.

The other thing I do is let someone cry to me, but I sit and cry alone. It takes me time to process my thoughts or what I'm going through. I don't call or text anyone immediately when a problem or issue arises. Sometimes I don't say anything for weeks if I am having a hard time dealing with whatever it is. It's as if my brain and heart have met up and agreed to screw me over.

Do you think we were built with an internal conspiracy between our mind and heart that gets activated when our internal instincts are abandoned? Like a punishment of sorts? Regardless of what it is, then comes the work to unfuck myself. That's when I talk to one of three people. God bless them. They have their hands full with me.

Another issue is that I just don't like people in general. Yes, I know that I sound like a bitch for saying that, but it's impossible to like everyone, all of the time. If we have learned anything in 2020, it's that more people than not feel the same. Sometimes I don't even like myself. I drive myself nuts! In all likelihood, I'm going to get on your nerves, just as you will get on mine. We can totally have a great time together, but you'll know you are my person when I hit you with my truth. If I tell you to get off your high horse, then you are riding that high horse straight into my heart.

Ultimately, there is a balance between my personalities. They all take turns helping me adjust to the world around me. For instance, I'm not going to show my ass at a function (although I have on occasion), but we aren't going to swap BFF bracelets either. As I've gotten older, I realize how important it is for me to have a small group of people with whom I can run away. As a matter of fact, I often ran to my friend Carrie's house. The kids knew it was time to grab their toothbrushes when I told them where we were going.

Our lives get so complicated and rushed that it's imperative to have a safety net—vegging out with a girlfriend, watching movies in your pajamas, or having a full-on dance party in your living room after several bottles of wine. Being able to hit the Reset button on life qualifies you to be my people. I love my girlfriends, and they are the ones who make me a ride-or-die.

So many women in my life have been unforgettable. This is not to say that all of our experiences were the happiest of times. There are times I wish I could erase or at least forget. Then there are those times I was so drunk I don't remember them, and would like to know how things went south. But if things are meant to be, then there is no challenging the inevitable. Those lessons were going to be learned in one way or another. People who truly care about you aren't going to be spooked the first time an issue or conflict arises. True friends will be there to deal with it head-on, whether or not you or they like it.

My friend Theresa put it best when she said, "I'm kind of pissed at you for not telling us sooner." I was going through something—I don't remember what anymore—and that was her response when I finally spoke up. No sooner said than done, she started trying to fix me. Don't we all need people who will fix us?

I have failed at friendships many times over. There is one other person whom I still miss to this day. Things were just one bad event after another. She was so sweet, had a huge heart, loved her daughter like nothing else, and had a charismatic personality. Our time together was short-lived. My story will never change; neither she nor I were to blame for our current status: nonexistent. I still have so much love for her and her adorable blonde-haired, blue-eyed little girl. Maybe time will come back around, and we will be dancing in my kitchen again. Until then, I wish the best life has to offer for those two.

Now for the friendships that have often ended like a horrible B-rated movie. Our ideas and lives may not have synced, but I've learned so much from you. You helped to make me stronger. I've learned how awful a person I can be. Because of you, I know what I want, need, will and will not accept, and how to unfuck my craziness. I am humbled to have known you, and, realizing I will never have to deal with you again, I raise a glass. Bye, bitches!

Ride-or-Diers

Kelley is my very best friend. We met over the phone when I first moved to Tennessee. Her now ex-husband worked with mine as a soldier, and she was my point of contact for our company's family readiness group. Anyhow, she innocently called to welcome me to the area and the company, but asked for my husband's ex-wife! Yes, you are reading that correctly. She called asking for his ex-wife, and I told her she had taken the week off. To this day, Kelley will never let Arnie live it down, as it was his fault for not updating his information. As I look back on that call, I remember it as the time I unknowingly gained a sister.

There hasn't been one thing that I can think of that she and I have not gone through together. We have laughed, cried, been scared out of our minds, yelled and fought with each other, held a sick baby, seen death, dealt with pregnancies, walked through divorce, and all that comes in between. She is who will inherit our children should I die. She is who I want to share every facet of my life with. She is everything I'm not, and I mean it. She is feisty and eclectic. She has a strong voice that is very direct and unafraid of having a different perspective. She's a people person who wears so many hats and is extremely involved in her community. Kelley is my soul sister even when she needs to get off her high horse! Truth be told, she's kind of a big deal; at least to me she is. Kelley is my Elizabeth Taylor!!!

I have so many favorite memories with her. We used to celebrate every holiday when our kids were little. When I say little, I mean her oldest was three, she was three months pregnant, Hannah was two, and Samuel was one. We color-coded the parties and used special letters as a learning tool for the children. I babysat her oldest while she worked as a personal trainer at the local gym until the day before she gave birth to her second kid. We used my staircase as a slide, we danced on poles, we endured ten-hour car rides to enjoy mandatory family vacations, and she cared for my older kids when I visited our third baby in the neonatal intensive care unit (NICU). This woman taught me how to use a dishwasher at the age of twenty-four. The stories are endless, and that's how I want to keep it.

As with many great duos, we have had our share of fights. It usually starts off with one of us being self-absorbed because life has thrown us another curve ball, and the other is trying to give insight. There was a time that we stopped talking for a whole month. I was so lost. All I knew was that I didn't *want* my friend back; I *needed* her back. Then there was the one time that she was getting married, and we yelled at each other on the front steps of this high-end hotel. Now that moment was totally my fault. I felt completely overwhelmed with wanting things to be perfect for her, but I was so broke. So broke, in fact, that we literally skipped a house payment to go to the wedding. I totally made an ass of myself and told her to get off her high horse. I cried all night. The following morning, as she always does, she forgave me; we got ready and married her off. She's the Thelma to my Louise…without the dying part.

Fast forward, we both now have four kids each. They are all so strange, goofy, loving, and perfect in my eyes. In August of 2021, I was able to go see her and meet my sweet Charlotte, the youngest of the bunch. It was a week filled with giggles, Silly String, sidewalk chalk, snuggles, and lots of wine. I don't know that it could have been any better. In December 2023, my family loaded up our car, made the twenty-four-hour drive, and went to visit for a crazy five days, during which we finally got our group picture.

Kell, thank you for being everything I never knew I needed, even when we don't see eye to eye.

Then there's the squad, as we like to call it. Amanda, Carrie, Theresa, and I just all clicked. From the start, it worked effortlessly and still does. I've known Carrie the longest, but it feels as if the four of us were just formed out of thin air. I don't know about them, but, nine times out of ten, I only use our group chat. Whatever I say to one, I say to all. Whatever question I ask, stupid meme I send, moment I nag about, it goes out to all three of them at the same time.

My absolute favorite memory of us was our trip to the Kentucky Derby. It poured down rain on us in midfield. We were soaked, muddy, and couldn't give a damn. During our Atlanta trip, Paul and Paulina made their grand public debut. We all have distinct personalities that work well together. I would say we're like the Golden Girls; you cannot have one without the other three—I hope it stays that way.

The other special women in my life are all so different. I have been so blessed to have a spectacular group of women who make me whole. Each of them brings out something different in me. Some feed my hunger for raw laughs, others make me feel God's presence, and then there are those who are a grounding force when I'm in a tailspin.

I don't talk to any of them on a daily basis. Well, shit, some of them I haven't spoken to in months, if not years. Like my friend Jen. Time and distance didn't make her any less special. They're special to me for what they give me. They're in my heart for a reason as special and unique as they are. This is why I say it's so wonderful to be multifaceted. A fire doesn't burn with only one twig, so why would a fire burn within us with only one friend?

In the middle of writing this book, we moved from Tennessee to Texas (thank you, Army). I felt isolated and alone for a very long time because I lost my connection with so many people. A few women reached out, but although I was thankful, I was living in misery. I had never wanted to move back to my home state. The past I ran away from, the one I was healing from, the one that taught me that life sucked—it was back in my life.

I finally loosened up and got in touch with a friend whom I had met in Tennessee; she had moved to San Antonio some years prior. Then I reconnected with an old high school friend and the rest of the tribe. I was able to meet up with them the night before my high school friend married the love of her life. Since then, we have maintained constant connection. One that, I feel, time was unable to break. It was almost as if that part of life were simply on pause. I will obviously never know what they went through while I was gone, but I am so thankful that they are each in my life. These bitches are a whole mood and party with each text we send. This picture must have been taken in 1997 or 1998, and we still look this damn good!

Writing this chapter makes me miss so many friends. I often don't realize how much I do, or how important it is for me to have and keep these people in my life, regardless of their status: lifelong, short-term, or part-time friends, or those connected with my soul. At the end of the day, friendship is all about balance for me, and y'all make me a better person. It'll be interesting to see how the ladies I interviewed relate to the relationships around them.

Friends come in all shapes and sizes. They can be as cozy as an oversized cashmere sweater and leggings, sitting in front of a fire, or they can be the most constricting, itchy pair of SPANX you can imagine. I don't know that you can choose who walks into your life, but you can sure as hell choose who stays. As I said before, I am grateful for each person who has come into my life. I am blessed with the ones who stayed. I am free from the ones who left. I can also appreciate those who feel the same about me—both good and bad.

What do your friendships look like? Have you had your share of failures and successes? Who would you want back in your life? Are you willing to forgive someone who hurt you? No matter what your answers are, I challenge you to see yourself both in those you keep around and in those who are no longer in your life. Appreciate each of them for the lessons learned.

Chapter Two

Female Empowerment: What Does It Mean to You?

*Giving women a platform is important,
Giving yourself a voice is crucial.*

Let me start by saying, I'm not knocking any one way to empower women, but y'all won't find me burning my damn bra. First of all, those suckers are expensive! Even if you buy one at Walmart, you're going to spend twenty dollars on it. That's the equivalent of grabbing a twenty-dollar bill and lighting it on fire. Um, no, ma'am.

Then you got the issue of what my boobs look like after I've taken my bra off at the end of the day. I'm forty-one years old and have breastfed four kids. As soon as that clasp comes undone, my boobs look like the ears of a damn basset hound . Again, no, ma'am, it ain't happening. You'll also not find me in a vagina costume protesting anything. For that matter, I won't be holding a Slits, Not Dicks poster either. My husband is a retired infantry soldier; the vagina jokes are ruthless, endless, and have reduced my consumption of roast beef. Just saying.

All jokes aside, I think the epicenter of empowering others comes from the understanding of differences, finding strength in your personal beliefs, and respecting the views and values of others. Who would have ever thought that we would unite over a woman's right to vote, gay rights, and HIV awareness and that it would devolve into literally destroying people's property or careers due to a conflict of interest or difference of opinions in the years to follow? In my opinion, cancel culture is just the beginning of the end of freedom of speech. If living in the present times has taught me anything, it's to be open-minded and accepting of everyone (so long as they aren't causing harm to others).

I am fully aware of the vast types of demonstrations over the decades and the levels of intensity. My disdain for violent protests comes from my inner fear of physical violence. The other possibility is that I've never felt the need to fight that hard for something in which I believe. Would you say I was passive, ignorant, or privileged? My view is that I'm all three. My current view on politics is that we aren't as divided, racist, homophobic, hell-raising NRA members, or cop haters, as we're portrayed. Let's not be naive and say that there aren't those outliers who seem to get the most attention by being those things, but also, remember, the rest of us really try to find a balance.

Hate, in my humble opinion, is the demise of all civilizations because it encompasses many forms of greed. The million-dollar question is: How do we meet in the middle to effect real change for the benefit of all or most? Because, if we're being honest, most things in life aren't one size fits all. There are many complex issues we are facing today; cookie-cutter viewpoints won't be our solution. The other major issue is that our politicians (left and right) have gone rogue because their allotted $140,000 per year salaries, paid by the American taxpayers, are lining their pockets and allowing privileges in obscene ways. It's my belief that they want to keep us divided.

Let's use the hot topic of abortion as an example. *Roe v. Wade* was passed in 1973, and forty-eight years later it is still being argued. Not only that, but it was overturned in a stunning and unexpected decision by the United States Supreme Court in June 2022! Is there a middle ground on abortion? The far left and far right would say no. I happen to think we can find one, and it doesn't involve the government. Actually, I don't think anyone should have a say, other than the woman and her physician. I've heard arguments that the baby's father should have a say. That gets complicated so quickly, and I'm not one hundred percent sure where I stand on it.

One of the women I spoke with stated:

> *I don't regret having my abortion. I am so thankful I had the right and ability to go in and terminate a pregnancy that would have made my life and my current children's lives beyond stressful. There is not an ounce of doubt in my mind that I made the best decision for all involved at that time in my life.*

Others may not feel strongly about this woman's decision, one way or another, but I don't feel we should be so quick to cast aside anyone who doesn't view life or any topic as we do. I see abortion the same as I see end-of-life assistance. It's extremely personal, not for everyone, an irreversible decision, and one that can and will potentially leave eternal scars.

On these and other subjects, it would take a serious group of humans from all walks of life to consider every factor, including the safety of the men, women, and children, and to study the issues; we would have to rely on them to give those involved a voice. Oh, wait! Wasn't that the concept on which our democracy was founded? A group of people to create and uphold the laws of the land in order to ensure its people are afforded the opportunity for a safe, healthy, and free life? I also don't mean *free* as in *handouts*. I mean *free* as in the *freedom to choose* your own path and to create your own life as you see fit.

If COVID-19 taught us anything, it taught us that the select elite in government and medical science were willing to, and ultimately did, reset us to fit their ideology and line their pockets. If you don't see it or haven't read about it, you may want to come out of quarantine and stop living under your mask. I have seen the effects of COVID-19 firsthand, as have others. I'm also not saying it hasn't caused its own destruction. However, what I feel is clear is that it's not a good day when abbreviated agencies use things against us to force us to submit and to control us.

The stance that men cannot make legislation for women because they have a penis is also as ridiculous as saying a man can birth a child. I think we should reword it and specify that your god and misogyny should be left at the door before making and passing laws. Besides, who the hell was going to make female-friendly legislation before women started holding office and exposing their wealth of intelligence? The fact is that men have been in positions of power because women were considered less than or docile. Come to find out, that's far from the truth. Our country has had some brilliant and strong women who carved out the path for the rest of us to find our own destiny. Regardless whether I agree or disagree with trailblazing women, I still applaud their courage.

With so many topics to fight for, there will always be ideas and presentations galore. But what about our everyday fights? The ones in which we just need to get through the next few minutes? The personal struggles that we have with our own body image, personality, or external demands? Fighting to have a balance in life and not let others determine what and who we are? After all, strong women create strong victories. My heart goes to these moments. Have you had your heart break or feel so alone and lost that you didn't know how you were going to get past the next fifteen minutes, much less the next twenty-four hours? This is when I've needed the most support and love. Having friends, who are in all actuality my lifelines, resuscitate me is a precious treasure. Now, that's empowering.

The most frightening feeling I have ever experienced was complete and utter shock. Not the shock of, "Oh shit, I'm pregnant again, and I have a six-month-old," or the shock of getting a call from the school principal that your son is being suspended. I'm talking about the type of shock that changes the trajectory of your very existence. The one that leaves you not only speechless, but also emotionally void, with no idea of when or if you will ever feel again. This was when I desperately needed someone to breathe life back into me. When I needed someone to let me scream, cry, and contemplate murder without judgment.

If I'm going to be totally honest, there *was* a lot of judgment. I don't think it meant my friend (my one and only friend at the time) was listening to my story and talking crap—although, maybe she was. But I think she was genuinely surprised by my situation, and I don't blame her one bit. I couldn't wrap my mind around my situation, so how could anyone else?

In my world, this event was catastrophic because it was my mother who deliberately attempted to ruin my life, and by extension, that of my husband and children. I spent the next month and a half going through life in slow motion—painfully slow. It wasn't a life I would wish upon anyone. The tears never fell. The screams waited. The anger held back. I knew I was breathing, but suffocating at the same time. I felt nothing; it was as if I had been given anesthesia for my emotions and thoughts. At times, I wondered if that's how death felt. Was this the end of the happiness I had once felt and the beginning of endless pain to come? Looking back, I can't remember how I got through day after day.

What I do remember was the first time I felt something after this tragedy. We bought a dining table, and my husband and I were moving the old one to our breakfast nook. The table was heavy, I was weak, and it slipped out of my hands and landed on my ankle. Every negative emotion that lives in a human's repertoire came rushing out as if it were an angry tsunami hitting a shoreline, something that could be controlled by only God Himself. It was powerful and eerily frightening. Even though I was the one feeling it, I knew nothing had prepared me for that moment or the moment that set it all in motion. It took less than a second for the table to hit my ankle, the nerve response to hit my brain, and for me to finally explode. The tears flooded my eyes, and the screams finally found their way out of my body. I cried and screamed, off and on, for ten years. An ombre effect on my soul, but the color never faded back to the original color. I'll always be tainted.

Prior to this, I was certain I had been through more than my share of problems, and I had heard others talk about their trials. So, surely, I should have been prepared. Turns out, this was the *coup de grâce* of my life thus far. Let's all send out positive vibes or pray that nothing in the future surpasses this event.

Do you now understand my tagline? If you don't remember it from earlier, let me take a second to remind you. *Fuck it! It Can't Get Any Worse!* Makes sense for anyone when you think of the worst event in your life, regardless of how big or small someone else views it.

This may be a shot in the dark, but I'm going out on a limb here to assume you're skimming through the paragraphs to find out what happened to me. What could have been that horrific? Was I raped? Yes, but that wasn't it. Do I have a child who could have very well died at birth? Yes, but he didn't. Was I fired? Yes, but that wasn't it either. Did someone cheat on me? Yes, but it wasn't my husband. After much deliberation, I spoke with my family and decided this would be the one thing I would discuss as an overview and keep the details private.

Sorry to disappoint, but this *thing* was bigger than just me, and I'm not out to destroy anyone. Moreover, this is simply an event I still guard with my heart. It's okay to keep certain things unspoken for many reasons, and I feel it's important for each of us to trust ourselves to do just that. Trust when I say there is plenty for you to talk shit about as my story continues to unfold. For one, you'll learn that I don't have a relationship with my mother. I hope I can walk the line between truth and vengeance.

My mother and I have always had a strained relationship. If I had to guess, the main reason is that I'm so much like my father, and she wasn't his biggest fan, if memory serves me correctly. I was free-spirited, busy, inquisitive, and on the go. She was quiet, reserved, scared of everything, and passive aggressive. I saw her as weak, and that is the one thing I've never wanted to be. As the years progressed, I knew I couldn't trust her. I knew she didn't have my best interest at heart because she couldn't. There is no diagnosis that I can bestow on her, but I would say there are a couple of diagnoses that suit her quite well. She and I fought for many years, but I always tried to do the right thing. By that, I mean I tried to fix her problems. I didn't know at the time that it was impossible to do so.

For years, she would create a mess, and I would come in to clean it up. It was years of not being enough, being too much, fucking up, making her happy, pissing her off, and the cycle would repeat itself. After I left for Tennessee, several times she came stay with us because she had caused issues with her family. I used to tell my husband not to pay too much attention to her because she was a ticking time bomb. He never understood me and chalked it up to mom-daughter spats.

The biggest warning came from my favorite aunt (may she rest in peace). She told me to be very careful because my mother had on several occasions told her she blamed me for her divorce and that she would be sure to pay me back and make me feel her pain. That's right; my mother blamed me for her and my father's divorce. I knew that my aunt wasn't lying because I had already experienced my mother saying that to me directly and later laying the foundation for her spiteful and disgusting work. I shouldn't have been surprised when my mother attempted to make a sexual pass at my husband since everything else had failed.

Yup, that was the life-changing event. She has called me everything from smart and beautiful to a slut and a whore. That didn't bother me. Without telling me, she used my identity to get an apartment, turn on utilities, etc., and then failed to pay any of it, leaving me with the shittiest of credit. Not a problem. She encouraged me to enroll in college classes, and as repayment for living with us, she watched the kids when I had class. The second she got tired of it (usually as soon as it was too late to withdraw from classes), she went on a rant to remind me the kids were my problem, not hers, and then she would refuse to help. Cool. She, on many occasions, told my husband that I wasn't good enough for him, and he should leave me. Awesome.

I was okay with it. It hurt, but I didn't know a life other than this back-and-forth with her. This was who she had been my whole life. It wasn't until I caught her trying to make a pass at my husband that I knew I could no longer have her in my life—and I am still dealing, healing, and hurting from that. No one knew what growing up with her was like. No one understood my pain or perspective. I lost more than just my mother. I lost the relationship as I knew it with my grandmother. I lost myself. I lost any and all understanding of everything. Every once in a while, I saw my mother with my cousins, and she would be going above and beyond for them. It always left me wondering why I wasn't good enough for her. I lost my mother because of the things she did, not due to her death. Grieving her loss has been the most difficult process of my life.

Thank God for Kelley because I think she would have run my mother over with a car if I had asked. She was the one who shared her power with me when I had nothing left. I'm sure she had better things to do in life than to listen to my bullshit, but she did. A couple of years after meeting Carrie, we got close, and I opened up to her. She also shared her power with me. These two women pulled me out of the depths of hell.

We've all heard and read countless times that strength comes from within. Even the most powerful women on

Earth have a support system for those times that life comes knocking. Either way, I hope you have a better understanding of why those intimate moments of empowerment in our lives mean the most to me. Does any of this resonate with you? Have you shared your power with anyone, or have you been on the receiving end?

On a different level of empowerment comes the next step, the middle picture, if you will. What I call overall social empowerment. Why do people feel they have a right to tell each other how narrow or wide our paths or thoughts should be? Haters can't empower anyone, simply because they do not possess critical-thinking abilities. Yes, I fucking said it —no, I didn't call you or anyone else stupid. I reserve that right for special occasions. For instance, when my GPS gives me directions, and it thinks I know my cardinal directions, or when I'm looking for ice in the spice cabinet.

As I was saying, critical thinking is taught to us at a very young age, and in some ways—basic ways—we are born with it. Well, let's hope it was taught to us. According to Google, critical thinking is defined as "the objective analysis and evaluation of an issue in order to form a judgment." With everything in me I believe the key word is "objective." Are selfishness or being close-minded traits of a person who is looking for positive change or attempting to empower their cause? By definition, I would assume the answer is no because with those traits, you are simply encouraging same-minded people while alienating others.

Not actively listening is a problem. Yelling your stance is another. Shouting or forcing your point of view on someone who is in direct opposition results in making your point moot to all those you could have reached. Your point(s) could have saved humanity, but your delivery sucked. Therefore, we all lose. Lack of growth under any circumstance is losing. You see, whomever you were trying to reach has been shut down by your delivery, resulting in lack of persuasion and possibly the cementing of opposing beliefs as a negative response or reaction to your delivery of information. You lose because your ideas and thoughts are now falling on deaf ears, no matter how good they are. It saddens me to say this happens so often in today's times. I'm neither a stranger to it, nor an innocent bystander. I've been on both sides of the fence, which helps me realize how terribly wrong I was and how important it is for me to correct that poor behavior.

What about thinking critically? Would that help promote the idea of researching, investigating, or keeping an open mind about your life and the world around you? To think critically empowers your mind to further dive into the unknown. No one person will ever know everything, but if you share your knowledge and I share mine, we can discover endless possibilities. This would mean learning from the past and using it for a greater good. Not simply sitting in one place, blaming others, and victimizing yourself or others for the rest of your life. Whether it's personal or global history, it's ours for the taking to ensure our stories are not only told but learned from in their most pure and honest of versions.

Besides, what are we so afraid of? Are we afraid that our points of view are fragile or have too many inconsistencies, so we cannot respect those thoughts and choices and shoot down opposing views in order to shield ourselves from their bullets of intellect? Honestly, some of these bullets are made of foam and would never hold up in a fire fight. Others may hurt like a bitch, and, if so, that is a prime indication to do some soul searching to understand why. Ask yourself this: Is expansion of information ever wrong? I think not. I challenge you to learn more, understand more, ask more questions, and take the time to calmly have discussions with people of opposing views. That is another version of empowering someone and yourself!

So we have covered personal and intimate empowerment along with social empowerment. Now let's chat about empowerment that has made women a household name. Sandra Day O'Connor, Marie Maynard Daly, Ruth Bader Ginsburg, Harriet Tubman, Rosa Parks, Maya Angelou, Maria Elena Martinez (my personal hero), and so many more. The force of their endurance and passion, and their lack of "don't give a fucks," has changed our lives in ways I don't know we can ever fully repay. Imagine what our worlds would look like without these powerhouses.

Sandra Day O'Connor was the first woman to sit on the United States Supreme Court. My favorite quote by Marie Maynard Daly is that "successful people are those who failed and kept going." She was the first African American woman in the United States to earn a doctorate in chemistry. Ruth Bader Ginsburg will forever be remembered for her role in gender equality. Harriet Tubman was born into slavery and ended up changing not only her destiny, but that of many others. She was a brave woman who helped free slaves in the early 1900s as part of the Underground Railroad. The most widely remembered action of Rosa Parks was her refusing to give up her seat on a bus due to her skin color. Prior to this December 1955 event, she had already put the wheels in motion to combat racial injustice by joining the NAACP more than ten years prior. I'm going to save Maya Angelou for just a bit more.

My absolute favorite woman mentioned above is Maria Elena Martinez. She was born on July 23, 1933, and was one of six children. Her mother passed away when she was very young, so she took over the responsibility of raising her younger siblings. In 1952, she married her soulmate. They moved around quite a bit, as her husband was a construction worker for many years. As time went on, they had six children and settled in Austin, Texas. Her husband's sudden passing in October of 1995 left her alone to continue the life they had built with twenty-one grandchildren, forty-two great-grandchildren, and one great-great-grandson. She never remarried and has stayed faithful to her unwavering love for her deceased husband.

I am lucky enough to be one of the twenty-one grandchildren. My grandmother—or Ama, as we call her—has a fire in her that doesn't ever burn out. She's a fighter. Ama worked in the cafeteria of a local high school for many years. After my grandfather passed away, she rode the city bus an hour to and from work each day until she retired. My grandmother would not only sew all the girls a matching dress or outfit, but would never miss a birthday card. Each card holding a dollar for each year of your life; my children always looked forward to them. Food was plentiful, there was always an available chair, and when times were hard, fifteen people at a time would manage to make her three-bedroom, one-bath house a home. How? Because *she* is home. Now I will say she has a sharp tongue and quick sass. Has never backed down from an argument and prays her Rosary every night without fail. You know—a little holy, a little hood.

You may ask why I've spent so much time writing about her. Well, because I learned so much about unconditional love, grit, and resiliency from her. When I got pregnant the first, and then the second time, I was unmarried. That was a huge no-no to her, but she moved forward *with* me, instead of against me. When I met my husband, he asked her for my hand in marriage. I had a difficult pregnancy and birth with our third child, so she moved to Tennessee to care for me and help with our older two. She stayed with the kids while my husband and I traveled an hour to and from the hospital to see our son in the NICU. She never once complained. She also stayed with me nine months after he was born because my husband deployed back to Iraq. Every moment she held my hand, every time she rubbed my head, every word of advice, every tear she wiped, and every second I spent with her empowered me to be more. How could anyone live up to her?

I wanted to finish off with Maya Angelou. As we all know, she has played many roles, but she wrote a poem entitled *Alone*, a part of which goes like this:

> *Now if you listen closely*
> *I'll tell you what I know*
> *Storm clouds are gathering*
> *The wind is gonna blow*
> *The race of man is suffering*
> *And I can hear the moan*
> *'Cause nobody, but nobody*
> *Can make it out here alone.*
> *Alone, all alone*
> *Nobody, but nobody, can make it out here alone.*

I believe in my heart no words have rung truer. Her poem captures the heart and soul of empowerment. It embodies the essence of human instinct that requires us to bond with one another. I assume that even the most introverted of us need to be empowered by connection.

In all honesty, this was the hardest chapter to write. I struggled with words, phrases, and the idea of what it all meant to me. I'm not a die-hard feminist, but I most certainly want to champion the women of the world. My personal difficulty with empowering the few women I have met who needed it was the idea of getting behind someone who is self-centered or has become comfortable being the victim of their own life. I don't want to be a victim or a survivor. My story is just a story. Possibly worse than others, but not nearly as painful as the rest.

That isn't to say we shouldn't have moments of being self-centered. At every crossroad, it's imperative to evaluate which path to take with ourselves in mind. The same goes for being a victim. Shit happens in some of the most horrific ways, and other times in ways we never knew we were victims. We should recognize those times to fight back and become stronger. It's taken a long time for me to realize that strength comes in many forms. Most importantly, I want to see strength when I look in the mirror.

Look, we have all been through our own shit, some of us more than others. The people with whom I have a hard time are those who can't get off their soapbox. You know, the one-uppers who have been hurt more, screwed over more, taken for granted more than anyone else. Arnie taught me that no one but you can keep you from drowning in a puddle of water; all you have to do is stand up. Sometimes it's easier said than done, but he's so fucking right! We all have our own way of healing and taking the next step. When we do, we get to show the same support to others, and, in my personal experience, it usually mimics the way support was given to us. Or maybe it's just that way for me.

The other ones who can really piss me off are the ones who are "educated" and belittle others. Having a degree is an accomplishment. Having more than one is something to be applauded. When I was younger, I thought having an education higher than a high school diploma was required to make me relevant.

In recent times, I've known three women who've earned their doctorates. Three women who are mothers, wives, full-time employees, friends, daughters, etc. However, there's a huge difference in the way one of them carries themselves. I one hundred percent believe they should have pride in such an accomplishment, but two of them are truly humble. They aren't going to bow down or downplay their intelligence or accomplishments, but they sure do carry themselves with grace. That makes me admire them all the more.

Hell, I knew someone a lifetime ago who had an associate's degree and thought they were the best thing that had ever happened to her basket-weaving class. Y'all, she couldn't go a conversation without telling me how fucking smart she was. So guess what I did about it? Yup, I lied to her. I told her I had a degree too, and it didn't make me any more special than she was. Yes, that happened, and it's another friendly reminder of the shit show that I am. I'm telling you, I have made terrible choices in my past. You know, if she had been mentioning her intelligence during a relevant conversation, then maybe I wouldn't have snapped. But why did she, or does any other woman with a doctorate, have to use their accomplishment to fuck with people and act superior?

Why do some people feel the need to tear other people down to make themselves feel better? That's an internal struggle that requires real attention. Turns out that I learned so many valuable lessons from a woman who only made it out of elementary school. My ama has always been the hardest, strongest, most able woman I know. This little eighty-nine-year-old lady will and can beat them all. I love how she doesn't back down from an argument, but when you make a point, she acknowledges it. I could go on and on about her, but that would be a book in itself. Point is, your education doesn't mean much when you treat people like shit. Get over your pompous ass.

The true rock stars are the women with wild ideas who may or may not fail, but always try! The ones who paved the way—even if it's just a foot—and show others. No secrets about who, why, or how. Just, "Here ya go; this is how I did it." I love seeing women who have shed those tears, yelled out in despair, but have come flying out of the flames! I like to admire the scars of others. How incredible is it to know that your scars aren't much different than those of the woman standing next to you at the checkout counter? She has been through something, maybe a lot of somethings, and is still standing in her own light to carry on. She carries herself as the brilliant person she is, someone who didn't accept no for an answer!

I watched a show on Netflix, and one of the main characters was asked how she sends the elevator down to other women so that they can get to the top as she did. This really made sense to me. How do we help others when we get to where we're going, or even as we're getting there? In my perspective, I try to tell my story. Like this book. Not every detail or name is divulged, but you get the point. I would hate for someone to walk blindly down my path if I can make a difference.

I have a friend whom I admire so much that I would like for our daughters to have traits like hers. She is intelligent and funny, tells it like it is, takes risks, loves big, sincerely apologizes, and accepts an apology. She is cautious, but not closed off. She has found herself and makes no apologies for it. She gives to others, but works her ass off for what she wants. She takes the time to learn from others' perspectives without (too much) judgment. I feel that what she is now comes from her years of trial and error. It also comes from being supported and supporting others. Now she's a momma to a sweet little baby bear who will surely grow into a wonderful man.

I know there are many ways to empower others, but in my little world, it's in the smallest, most difficult moments that we need others' unwavering support the most. We can gather, yell, protest, and move mountains, but we start moving mountains one shovel at a time. Ultimately, let's not forget to empower the most important person in our lives —ourselves. Why? Because we fucking rock and deserve it!

At the end of the day, we all have the power to make positive changes in life. Sometimes it's the smallest act of kindness to a stranger. Sometimes it's writing or passing legislation to improve the lives of the masses. How do you empower yourself or others? Do you have benchmarks for achieving your final goal? Are you pleased and satisfied with the legacy you are leaving when you look in the mirror? Could it be different? If there is a change you would like to see, what steps are you willing to take to achieve it? Kindness, understanding, compassion, and communication are the cornerstones for the fortress we are all building.

Chapter Three

Dreams: Goals, Fantasy, or Reality

Oh, man! This one was difficult to write. I have the capability to ruin a wet dream, so accomplishing anything in life is just stupid. Not only am I a procrastinator and a brat, but also I'm lazy. There, I said it. I'm lazy. Instant gratification is my jam! Then there's the fact that I'm terrified of failure and hyperfocused on negative responses, which leads to a downward spiral and to perfection being even further from my fingertips. My dreams and goals are also less popular than most. You know, I dream of a clean house. I dream of a beautifully manicured lawn. I dream of far-off vacations. The reality of my dreams is that I have four kids and three dogs, so the house will never be clean. I have literally killed a cactus. I'm afraid of flying. Not doing so well, huh?

For as long as I can remember, I only wanted to be a mom and wife. It was that simple for me. The other ideas were being an OB/GYN or marrying the head of the Mafia. No, really, I was stuck somewhere in between wanting to take care of mommies and spending money Mafia that came to me from unknown sources. As unrealistic as that was, I went with it for a while. I didn't grow up being told or reminded that I could accomplish anything. My mother was surprised I graduated high school and told me I just needed to get married so that I could be someone else's problem. In her defense, I think her thought process was just a product of her upbringing and environment; that's giving her some credit.

Besides, what did it mean to accomplish an idea or desire? I grew up seeing kids make first chair in band, cheer for years, play softball throughout high school, and make National Honor Society. But *how* did they do it? This wasn't something I could answer until many years later when our kids were (still are) going through their obstacles. The thought of doing homework annoyed me, and I didn't know how to be a friend, so team sports were out of the question. Looking back makes me a little sad, if I'm honest. Then I must remember what I tell my kids all the time—everyone in the world can give up on you, but you can't give up on yourself. Would it have made a difference had someone told me that at ten years old? Now I just sound like a whiny-ass quitter.

Years have rolled on, and I'm happy to report that I've learned a few things. Dreams, goals, and reality are, in fact, made of the same thing; they're just on different points of the spectrum. Take, for example, my dream of becoming a doctor. It stayed a dream because I had no discipline to take actions. Those actions would have made for attainable goals. Reaching those goals would have made it a reality. After truly understanding what I most wanted in life, I set the wheels in motion. I had sex! I'm just kind of, sort of kidding.

However, at the ripe age of twenty-two I had my first baby. I remember crying uncontrollably the first time I held her, knowing in that moment dreams do come true. Although our circumstances were less than ideal, she was my dream that became my reality. Here's the catch: you don't know what you're asking for until you've got it. It's nothing anyone could have prepared me for. The romantic notion built in my mind and heart was fulfilled, but the unexpected hardships kept me grounded.

Let me point out the obvious. I know I didn't bust my ass in college for years on end to achieve my dream. I know I didn't get rejected day after day to become a world-famous model. But this was *my* dream. My goal. My happiness all wrapped up in the first breath of this tiny human. Being a mother is the one thing in life at which I cannot fail. My dream that turned into reality will be voting, contributing to society, and someday raising my grandchildren. How scary is that?!

My favorite part of dreams is that they are such an intimate part of who we are. Sometimes we voice them to anyone who will stand still for five minutes. Oftentimes, we keep them quietly in our hearts to manifest in magical ways. I love to hear about plans for those retiring. Or the dream, thoughts, and planning of a new business. I wish more people spoke of their trials, errors, and failures when they spoke about their successes. Some may think it goes without saying, but I feel it's not emphasized enough. Success is art, and art is to be appreciated, right? You couldn't have a masterpiece without each brushstroke. Our brushstrokes are the failures and milestones of our lives and successes.

How do you react to your children's dreams? Do you think Catherine, Princess of Wales, dreamed of becoming a real-life princess? When supporting your children's dreams, do you sign them up for every class of every interest they have? Do you coach them from the sidelines? Do you let them ask for you to play catch, or vice versa? I took a hands-off approach, to a certain extent. I waited for the kids to ask me to play a sport or put them in a lesson. They had the opportunity to change it up; however, they were required to finish the season.

It was very important for us to teach our kids the value of their word and what it means to be a teammate. This is the same for school. You don't have to be the best, but you must show up and give your best. There will always be days, classes, or sports that just don't go right. That doesn't mean you failed. That means you're just having an off day, or it's just not your cup of tea. The other thing we have taught was a participation trophy is not needed. You don't need a slap on the ass every time you get a right answer or help your team to victory. My favorite award that our kids bring home is Most Improved.

I knew a woman who had two girls, and she dragged them from school to tutoring, to sports, to private trainings, to church, and then to more sport-specific activities. I was tired for all of them! I mean, her girls really were kind, smart, and athletic. Now they are off at college, putting everything they learned to good use. She always came across as being the best, having the best, and striving for the best—best was the only option. She and her husband were, and are, great parents, I just saw and did things differently.

Most Improved may not have been acceptable to them, but I adored seeing our children start in one place and work their asses off to grow and learn. Those trials and growing pains are nothing to scoff at because the only thing worse than a sore loser is a shitty winner.

Ask yourself this: What do you really get from life if you start at the top? Have you ever sat back at the end of the day and relished a small victory that's part of the bigger goal? What is your greatest award? Who believed in your dream with you? Is there a moment that made you feel as if you, or your child(ren), were on the right path?

Our third child is moderately to severely deaf and must wear hearing aids. To add to his hearing disability, he has significant intellectual delays, is missing a foot of intestine due to gastroschisis, and had Wolff-Parkinson-White syndrome, which has since been ablated.

Oh, but you should see this kid on a football field! His face lights up, but in a mean-mugging way. His alter ego, T-2, explodes from within on game day. He lives life flipping from one football-news broadcasting station to another. He reviews plays during the offseason, shows up to as many showcases as we can afford, and keeps up with workouts all on his own. Hell, this fool ran ten miles the day after Thanksgiving.

His dream is to play collegiate football at the University of Texas at Austin and then be drafted by the NFL. His mind fills with ambitions of both his big brother and him playing ball for different teams, and we parents have to choose which of their teams will win the Super Bowl. The kid is also a shit talker. Like, no joke, a referee once flagged him with a penalty for shit talking another player after a great tackle. His tagline is "THAT'S WHAT YOU GET!" With all the odds against him, he has some raw talent, and we will be fighting every step of the way to help him achieve his dream. God willing, we will all hear, "Tackle made by Michael Nino," or "Ball was intercepted by Michael Nino," while watching a Rose Bowl or playoff game.

I could be selfish and say that he deserves every dream to come true, after all that he's been through, but don't we all? How cute is it to look back on this tiny child asleep in his car seat after his first-ever football practice in full pads?! Watching his dreams unfold is something so special and should be cherished. Your dreams should be cherished just as much. As I tell you that you and your goals matter, I'm reminding myself of the same thing. On to finishing this book!

The most beautiful thing is that there is no right or wrong with dreams. There is not one path to your goal, nor an expiration on achievement. The statement I raise our kids on is worth repeating: Everyone in the world can give up on you, including your dad and me, but you can NEVER give up on yourself. It really is true. No one can lose weight for you, no one can take a test for you, no one can suck on your road to success…except for you! If anyone else did it for you, it would be their accomplishment and sweet rewards, not yours. You do you, and tell those naysayers to fuck off!

So raise your dirty martini, and cheers to all our dreams, goals, and successful realities!

Chapter Four

Career: How Has It Worked for You?

The shortest answer in this book for me: I don't have a career. Some kids grow up wanting to be a doctor, fireman, soldier, movie star, or whatever. My kids have ambitions for themselves, and my husband talked about what he wanted to be when he grew up. We've already covered what I wanted and later got. Is anyone doing what they wanted? Is it what you expected? Did you choose your own path, or did life choose for you?

Had you asked me a few years ago, I would have told you that I needed so desperately to get a college degree. It was more out of my own insecurities. I've met so many women with degrees, careers, and intelligence that I put myself down. I felt inadequate and inferior when in their presence.

"Hi, I'm Karen, and I'm a biochemical engineer."

"Hi, Karen. My name is Mindy Jo, and I'm a mom."

It took a *long* time for me to realize that Karen's journey was different than mine, and that was okay. We wanted different things, accomplished different things, and can admire each other for our different strengths. The heartwarming thing is that we can also support each other in our struggles.

I was talking to a dear friend, and she said her mother once felt the same. Her mother was raising one child who would become a social worker and another, a radiologist, while married to a lawyer. My girlfriend said her mother was the strongest person she knew because she allowed her children to shine and be who they were meant to be. Maybe she said this to me because she knew I was struggling. Either way, I realized then that there was room for all of us. Career or not, we all play an important role. And if Rona didn't throw in our faces what an essential worker is, then nothing will. It also highlighted how important teachers and stay-at-home parents really are.

Kick off your career in high school or wait until you're fifty. Focus solely on one thing or branch out and change your mind. Want different? Take different steps to get there. Whatever you do for a living, it's important.

Chapter Five

Relationship: Shag, Marry, Kill

Like so many of us, my tearstained pillow has many tales she keeps secret for me. If she could, she would remind me of desperate times, moments of screeching in her, face-first, with excitement about dreams that had come to fruition, and sleepless nights. She would remind me that regardless of how I fell asleep, the sun rises with renewed promises. That God has given her to me to lay my worries on and lift myself out of bed to try again. Some days have been harder than others, as I am positive we have all experienced. Since July 2, 2004, I've shared her with this guy I didn't want to meet, but I undoubtedly know it's been the best I have ever felt in my life.

Truthfully, I had no business involving myself with that guy or anyone else. I met my husband at the most troublesome of times. I was a single mom of two very young babies (fourteen months and six weeks old) when I left the only life I knew. I was born and raised in the tiny border town of Del Rio, Texas. My life was in shambles by the time I was twenty-three. My parents were going through a bitter and ugly divorce, my little brother was off at college, doing whatever college kids do, sperm donor was causing new and innovative problems, and I was trying not to crumble under the pressures of life. To say I was broke and broken is an understatement. Over the following six months, life didn't get easier; I just learned how to deal with it. I was making plans, trying to keep my head above water, and giving my kids all that I could with the little I had. During that time, my grandmother was the pillar of strength that I so desperately needed.

On a random, hot June afternoon, my cousin's husband told me he wanted to introduce me to one of his friends, and it was a hands-down *no* from me. He says, "You'll like him! He's in the Army."

I said, "He must clean bathrooms in the Army. No!" He continues to tell me how his friend had made sergeant and what a badass he was. All I could respond with was, "Okay, then he cleans bathrooms really well." With all his attempted convincing, my only thought was still no. For perspective, the only thing I knew about the Army was what I had seen in commercials and a Pauly Shore movie. After our verbal tug-of-war, we both laughed and went our separate ways.

As an aside, when I told my would-be husband this story, he laughed, and it's remained a running joke to this day.

That weekend, my cousin and her husband had a birthday party for their oldest son (who's grown into such a marvelous young man). Our meeting was a brief one—quick introduction, hello, goodbye, no fireworks to mention—and we both went on with our day as if on different planets. Day turned to night, and after taking my kids home and putting them to bed, Ama insisted that I return to keep my cousin company. Tired and reluctantly, I did as I was told.

Aside number two: Looking back, this feels as if it were a romantic comedy with sappy music in the background and a wide shot of the lead actress oblivious to her future.

Once everything died down, all that was left were four adults talking and laughing; it is still one of my favorite moments spent with my cousin. Over the course of the night, I noticed how he was a man's man, holding it down with the wildest of them, yet maintaining respect for the women who were there. It was quite refreshing.

Spoiler Alert! We had our first kiss that night! Eek! Can you hear the giggle rolling off your page?

We also stayed up until nine o'clock in the morning, talking about nothing and everything. No, we didn't hook up! Y'all need to slow your roll. I had enough Catholic guilt, knowing I missed Mass that morning. My walk of shame may not have been sex-fueled, but it came with shame from just thinking of the disappointment my grandmother would feel. I thought she was going to have some words with me, but, instead, she saw my glow.

This became a whirlwind romance that made for a great week! Yes, folks, one week. He was on leave from the Army while he moved from one duty station to another. We just happened to meet the last week of his leave. The night before he left, he asked me to be his girlfriend. Things moved very swiftly from that moment. I moved in with him six weeks after meeting, and we got married six weeks after that. We have my cousin and her husband to thank for making this happen! We wouldn't have the family we do if it hadn't been for them.

Who can resist a love story like that, right? Honestly, looking back at our marriage, we have been blessed, lucky; the universe aligned, or something, because we are still together. Or was it magic and unified heart chakras? Truth is, it became what we put into it. As much as I believe in God,

He doesn't make the decisions that would make or break our relationship. In fact, our journey has taught me just as much as motherhood has. There is no secret. There is no magic wand. There is only talking, listening, and trying every day. Eventually, that turns into communication, understanding, and respecting each day as a gift.

When we got married, I had a two-year-old and a soon-to-be one-year-old, and I was knocked up, hormonal, and wearing a black dress. I was at the point in my pregnancy that I looked fat, not pregnant, so nothing fit. We show up at the justice of the peace's office on a sunny Friday morning after rushing out and driving like crazy people. Why? Because what pregnant woman with two babies isn't running late?

Anyhow, picture this: Arnie is holding Samuel in one arm and me in the other. The justice of the peace (JP) is giving his routine speech about how marriage should not be taken lightly. (I know he had more to say, but I don't remember any of it.) I am so consumed with trying to catch Hannah, who is running around the room and playing, that I am not paying attention to the ceremony. (Thankfully, we were the only ones there.) To add insult to injury, Hannah innocently lifts the JP's robe! Why? Because she is two! So here we are, Arnie holding Samuel, me reaching and pulling for Hannah, and Arnie not letting go of my hand so we can say our vows.

We finally made it through the fifteen-minute ceremony, which really felt like an all-day event. We were hitched on October 8, 2004, followed by a lovely reception at IHOP.

My "wedding" was nothing similar to what I had imagined growing up. At a young age, I wanted the fairy tale—a princess gown and adoring people gazing at me in awe. Then I became a teenager and couldn't think of a better muse than the bride in the Guns N' Roses video "November Rain." Now, that was the way to go!

I was honestly eight inches too short and about forty pounds too heavy for greatness like that. My black dress with cream polka dots just had to do. Not only did I use it as a wedding dress and maternity dress, but I've also worn it to work several times over the years. Can you imagine me walking into a psych hospital wearing a fancy, high-low wedding dress to work? Those fuckers didn't need any more ammunition to take away my badge and leave me with the patients.

As years have passed, my view on marriage has changed dramatically. I was convinced that my previous relationship didn't work because it was proven that I had premarital sex. No one was buying the immaculate-conception idea. You know, as long as you're not pregnant, people don't actually know you had sex, right? I was raised with the idea that you had to be married, with a certificate in tow, for God to bless you with a fruitful marriage; only then would you live happily ever after. Wasn't that a crock of shit! The lies we tell our kids will, in fact, catch up to us. My perception of love, commitment, and loyalty was screwed, to say the least.

What I realized was that my previous relationship didn't work because he was a lying, cheating, manipulative sack of shit. We could have had fifty marriage licenses or renewed our vows every month, and nothing would have changed. I was immature and naive; he was totally controlling and the worst human. It would have never worked. It took years for me to understand when and where the fault lay. The blurred lines and lack of emotional intelligence made for a time of many mistakes and lessons to be learned. Understanding life and relationships made things all too clear. Even if it took forty-two years and counting.

I should have known that karma would pay me a visit in my second relationship. My first boyfriend was sweet, patient, loving, quiet, and humble. I was the total opposite. I was harsh, loud, needy, obnoxious, a lying sack of shit, selfish, and just plain horrible. You know, everything I now hate. The years I spent with him weren't in vain on my part. I loved him, but I didn't love myself. That translated into all the vile things I was and he didn't deserve. The very last time I spoke with him was after I was married. I called to say how truly sorry I was and how much I had learned. This wasn't a moment in which I was looking for forgiveness—we were past that. It was just a broken person realizing her faults and owning them. I'm sure he was shocked when he heard my voice, and the one-sided conversation lasted less than sixty seconds.

That last phone call didn't change anything, really, but it did give me closure. It didn't change the hurt or pain I put him through, and it will never change how much his family hates me—rightfully so. I think it was just me owning my shit. Owning the wretched person I had been. As if I were shedding my skin to try again. Selfish? Probably. Did I let go? Absolutely. There are many characteristics that my husband and he share. However, the biggest difference is that my husband has a very strong and dominant personality. My husband keeps me grounded when I spin out of control—something I'll need my whole life that he does exceptionally well.

Nothing can make someone committed. No one can be made to be loyal. A marriage license is just a legality to protect, and sometimes screw over, the couple at hand. At this point in time, I don't feel anyone needs to get married. Get a will if you have a legal issue or wish; that would be cheaper, right? I love weddings and cry at each one I attend. I just don't think we all have to fit into one description of commitment. Does it matter if you are married or not? Does love change because of a piece of paper? I honestly don't care what your status is. I couldn't care less whom you love. I don't give two shits about how you do relationships. Straight, gay, shag, virgin—we all deserve to love and be loved honestly and with respect. You other naysayers should be more flexible with your ideology. I'm not asking you to change it; just be more open to a life you don't have to live.

Now the fun stuff! Just because I'm married doesn't mean I don't shag or want to kill. I think shagging as if I were a crazy, drunken twenty-year-old on a spring break is necessary and almost vital to a relationship. I feel all the more connected to my husband when we wake up the next morning with a grin on our faces and relive it for a few minutes before getting our day started. I also like the goofing off and foreplay that the day brings. You know, grabbing his ass while at the grocery store, or having an inside joke that only you will know what that look or touch means. Yes, the anticipation. Will we make it to bedtime, or will we just have to get in a quickie because the playing has been so fun?

Our sex life didn't start that way, and it isn't on ten all the time. The first time we had sex was awkward; it makes us both laugh every time we look back on it. My past experiences with intimacy and sex had tainted my desires and curbed my expressions. It took time for me to feel safe enough to fully enjoy what my husband had to offer. Although so much time has passed, I sometimes catch myself back in a place of insecurity, shame, and worthlessness. Our sex life takes a downward nosedive during those times.

It's always Arnie's love, patience, and kindness that bring me back to him. The way he makes me feel safe again and never judges or disparages—he gives me the support I need time and again. Years of therapy hasn't been a total loss either.

I also want to kill him some days. He drives me nuts when he bites a metal fork or spoon. When he is harassing the kids to the point of frustration. Ugh, it drives me fucking crazy when he questions me because he doesn't like how I'm doing something or wants me to change what I'm doing. As if he is dropping subtle hints! No, motherfucker! Like for fuck's sake! Just say, "Hey, dumbass, I like my shit this way, not that way." Then I will gladly hand over the task at hand and sit my fat ass on the sofa with a glass of wine. He's also a slow learner, so it took me years to break his habit of using metal utensils on my Teflon cookware! The cookware part is true, but he happens to be one of the most intelligent people I've ever met.

Those were little things that are minor annoyances in the grand scheme of things. Our biggest fight is that he's a flirt in the biggest way! I call him *"mi diente,"* in Spanish, which is "my tooth," strictly translated, but I mean it in a different way. I call him that because he has a huge smile and a boisterous laugh. It took us a long time to understand our boundaries with this part of his personality. The fact is that he has a big personality, which attracts others, and he very much enjoys being the center of attention.

I normally don't mind, but every once in a while, he teeters on a line until his drunk ass loses his balance. I understand the idea of working with the opposite sex, making friends, or just being friendly in general. But I'll be damned if he thinks some bitch is going to take center stage, whether I'm present or not! Fuck that shit!

Arnie has a couple of double standards that would make any feminist cringe. Then I have to remind myself that he is a father to two girls, and there's no limit to what he would do for them. He is really hard on both our sons, and although his expectations are wonderful, his delivery is sometimes questionable. Again, if I want our sons to be the epitome of masculine that I find attractive in my husband, then I need to let him raise our sons in a way that allows them to reach that goal. Nine out of ten times, we agree on what we want the outcome to be. Nine out of ten times, we disagree on how to get there. Patience and communication have been our saving grace, and that took exceptionally long to learn.

He has his flaws, and I most definitely have mine. Jealousy and possessiveness don't help. I put jealousy and possessiveness on the map. I've never been one to share my toys, and he is no different. I can say I feel the same about our kids. They all belong to me. Period. Additionally, I'm a control freak, petty, and ridiculously selfish. Not a pretty combination. I hold grudges and forgiveness isn't my strong suit.

Writing and thinking about it, why would anyone want to be around me, much less be married to a headache like me? I don't know, but I'm thankful he sticks around.

Almost without fail, he makes me coffee every morning before leaving for work, and I get cranky when he doesn't. He calls me almost every single day on his way home from work. There are days I'm so consumed that it frustrates me to answer the phone. Then the days he doesn't call me, I'm annoyed because what could he possibly be doing or to whom can he possibly be talking that he didn't call me? He always has a hug and kiss for me as soon as he walks through the door—even when it's just a peck because he is running to the bathroom.

I can always count on Arnie to help raise our children. It's probably my favorite thing about him. When the kids were little, he never shied away from cleaning up vomit, changing diapers, reading a book, teaching them to ride a bike or throw a ball. He was Hannah's Prince Charming. He was Samuel's superhero. He was Michael's sports all-star. Katherine thought he was magical. Not much has changed.

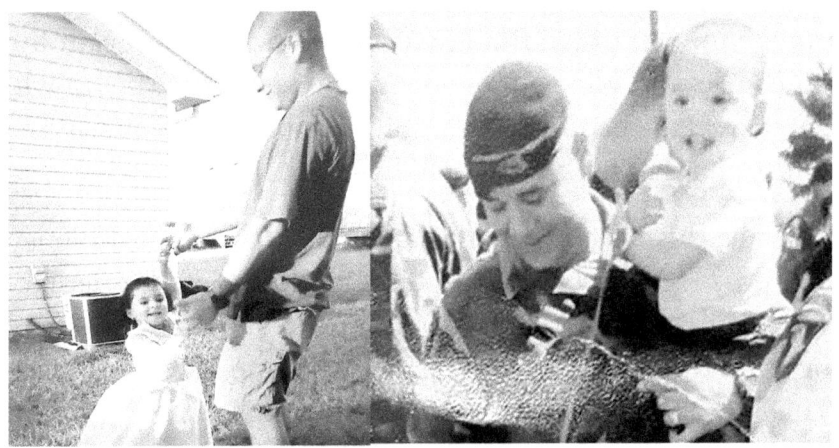

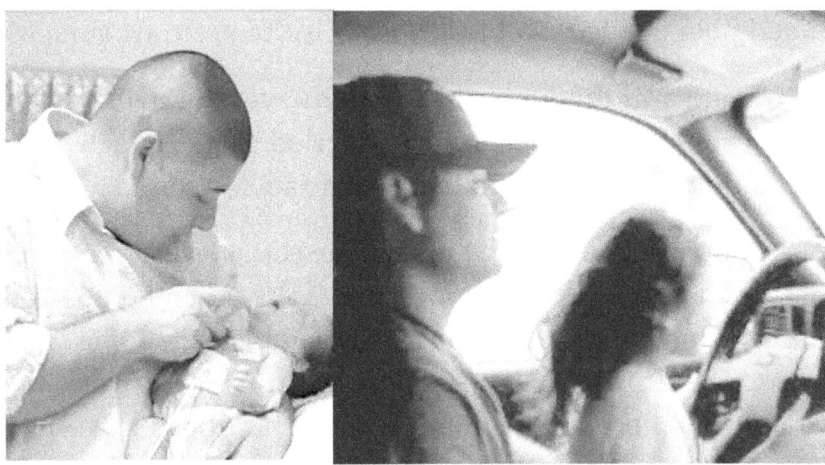

Our lives went from lullabies and babywearing, to having any conversation the kids can come up with. Yes, all the conversations. His kids are absolutely the most important thing in the world to him, so he's a no-holds-barred kind of guy with them.

It's nearly impossible to live with me, and not want to hurt me. I never claimed I was sane. I think I'm his right of passage into heaven. You know, his lifelong cross to carry—the very lucky cross. I am cranky, moody, and obnoxious, but I could be worse. He is a flirt, he doesn't express feelings well, and he has been a hell-raiser, but he could be worse. I may not cross the few lines that my husband set forth, but I sure do dance on them. He has a right to feel angered or hurt when I do that. He has the right to keep me in the doghouse from time to time, and I have the right to do the same.

We are a very passionate couple, so we love hard and fight hard. He is the most playful adult I know—sometimes annoyingly so. Arnie may be all brute strength and a beer- and whiskey-drinking, hard-ass, shit-talking motherfucker, but he makes me fall in love with him over and over.

For instance, seeing him play with our six-month-old on the floor. I fell in love with the man who sang lullabies to an infant in the NICU, night after night, for a month, before deploying and leaving his sick baby. With the man who lets our daughters paint his toenails. He takes the time to teach our kids how to change the oil in our vehicles and mow the lawn. I love that he has *never* just babysat our children. I love the man who quietly gives me a kiss every morning before leaving for work. The man who, at random, pulls me into his arms, looks me in the eyes, and kisses me with passion, even after eighteen years of marriage. He pays attention to the needs we each have.

I could go on and on. His dedication to our family is unwavering and cannot be broken by any outside source. I pray that never ends. I think he was born to be a father, giver, and provider.

It didn't go unnoticed how well he adapted and took care of two babies with little effort. This one will always be the greatest gift he gave me. The four of us went through so much while creating our family. Arnie remained steadfast while we navigated what was being thrown at us. We made it out of that storm, and he has now adopted both kids. It's as he told the kids—his love and actions won't change with a piece of paper; it's just a legality. They both insisted on going forward with it. They told him it was a way to honor him as the father he had always been, and they would be proud to carry his last name. How do you beat that?

I've been a terrible person at times, and I'm sure Jesus will have some choice words with me when I meet Him, but how did I get lucky enough to have a man come into my life for all the right reasons? I'm not sure, to be honest, but I'm going to keep accepting this blessing every day that God grants.

I don't ever want to take Arnie for granted because we have been close, a time or two, to losing it all. We have had our moments of destruction that have left us hanging by a thread. There's an old saying: "If the Army wanted you to have a wife, they would have issued you one." We all know marriage is difficult, but Army life isn't conducive to a healthy relationship. The statistics are overwhelming with divorce, affairs, and domestic violence. As I previously stated, my husband was infantry; he has seen his fair share of war. It's not just deployments and redeployments that make it difficult. It's the training cycles and schools. He was stationed in El Salvador for eighteen months, and that tested our marriage the most.

In my eyes and understanding, I expected the stress and strain. I was new to it all when we got married, but it seemed obvious. What wasn't obvious or explained was the hectic schedule he would keep. How difficult it would be to raise children while one parent was gone ninety percent of the time. What a relationship looked like or how it functioned when there was nothing but physical distance and no communication. When I say physical distance, I mean states, if not countries, away. When I say no communication, I mean phone calls were maybe ten minutes long, two or three times a month, when we first started out.

I kept the emails we sent to each other during our first deployment, as if they were old love letters. My favorite email to him was telling him we were having a baby boy. I remember sending that email with so much love and excitement, yet also with much hesitation, reservation, and heartbreak. The email and conversation that followed let him know his firstborn child would have his life tested as soon as he took his first breath. I cannot imagine what he must have felt, receiving that news while war weighed so heavily on his mind.

Nothing was easy about our lives. He and I have very different points of view on nearly all aspects of life, and being apart didn't help. I learned not to trust the Army or the wives' club. I learned to figure things out for myself. I learned that no one was coming to rescue me, so I better get my shit together as fast as possible. It worked. In fact, it worked so well that the dependency I think my husband thought I was going to have never fully developed. That was difficult for him because he was no longer in control, as he had been his whole life prior to me. We bumped heads like two full-sized rams in mating season.

Sometimes it was bitter and ugly. I've asked for a divorce, and so has he. It just happened to work out that we never wanted a divorce at the same time. So in those times, we reminded each other about the kids we'd promised to love and raise together. It was hard giving up on our family, regardless of what we were going through.

When we first got married, the conversation on PTSD wasn't at the forefront of the news or medical providers. I didn't understand the mood swings, but I also knew not to let our kids wake him up when he fell asleep on the sofa. I would do that by tugging on his big toe—while standing well away from his upper body—because I never knew if he would wake up swinging. The kids often slept in bed with me while Arnie was gone. That would come to an end when he was home because I didn't know if the nightmares would manifest in a kick, punch, or him pinning me down. He always felt terrible after I woke him up. These episode—as I call them—didn't last very long. The first month of his redeployment was always the hardest. The year leading up to retirement wasn't the easiest either.

Even during those months of readjusting to life, he found moments of peace. It was my duty to find ways to give him that peace, and sometimes I failed. There were times I was infuriated at how he wanted to parent our kids as if they were his soldiers. Sometimes I got angry at the mess left behind when he packed. Sometimes I was just tired of not feeling supported because he was too busy supporting his soldiers and their families. Hell, sometimes I was annoyed with him for no real reason, to the point that the way he chewed ice bothered me. It took me a while to understand that all of this was considered normal by Army standards. Arnie's strength and resilience impresses me, but it often leaves me wondering what is really going on inside his mind. I don't think I'll ever truly know.

Fast forward several years to his departure to El Salvador. Those eighteen months would unknowingly become the demise and rebirth of our family. A time that changed everything we had come to know about each other. I won't lie and say it doesn't hurt when I think about it, but I will say that we were left with two choices: grow together or finish growing apart. This meant all six of us—not just us as a couple.

Thank God, Arnie and I chose each other yet again. This time, we didn't only choose our kids, but we chose each other the way we did when we first met.

My perspective is my reality, so it was incredibly easy for me to know he was working and had a heavy, full plate on his hands, *but* all I could see were the fancy dinners and galas. Weekends at the beach, football games, and barbecues with his neighbors. I was stressing over working full-time, taking care of our four kids, and trying to stay sane and out of AA. We lost any version of who we were as a couple, and as a family. He came home to see us about every two months, but it was just for a weekend. In my experience, those short visits caused a great upheaval; our family routine was thrown out of whack, and it was exhausting. This is not to say that I didn't love seeing him, but each visit was a blatant reminder that we were growing apart; time wasn't on his side with the kids either.

By the time one year had come and gone, we were just two people who shared four kids. The last six months came with unexpected changes and challenges. We had been in Tennessee for fourteen years, without experiencing the typical Army move every two or three years. Tennessee is where we raised our children. It was our home. And then Arnie was given orders to be stationed in San Antonio, Texas. Although it was our home state, no one but Arnie was excited—which, in fact, pissed me off all the more. How the fuck could he be so happy while the five of us were in shambles?

The kids and I, with the help of one of my favorite neighbors, got the house ready to sell. We loaded up our vehicles in early August of 2018 and set out to find a new place to call home. The animosity I had already been feeling grew substantially. I had all but given up on us.

When Arnie came back to the States, the kids and I had already packed, sold, and moved out of the house that had been our home. We had already made what felt like a pilgrimage to Texas, where he would be stationed for the last time. Our children left the only life they knew and were so very sad.

Me? I was angry as hell! I was pissed our kids were completely heartbroken. Our children worked their asses off to help me get our home sold. With every paint stroke, with every potential buyer, with every goodbye, our kids showed more strength and courage than I had never known, and there was *nothing* I could do to protect their hearts. I was angry having to come back to Texas. I feared everything I had run from fourteen years prior.

When Arnie finally made it back to us, the work we had in front of us was abundantly clear. I wasn't the only one with resentment, as it turned out. We fought daily and didn't sleep in the same room. The kids were facing their own thoughts and feelings about leaving their home, and here we were, making it all the worse.

Something you don't hear discussed is the evolution of separation between kids and their parents. The kids had lost just as much time with Arnie as I had, but this was their father. I think the pain hits differently. For perspective, Arnie left when Hannah was fourteen and a half. He made it back after her sixteenth birthday. That's a *huge* transitional period for any child-parent relationship, so it's just that much more complicated when you add Army life.

I honestly couldn't contain my hatred, and the day I picked Arnie up at the airport made it that much more noticeable. I remember sitting by the baggage-claim area, waiting for him to arrive. I called Kelley to ask her how eighteen months went by so quickly. I asked her whether I should run up to hug him in a fake, C-rated movie style, or just be myself. She told me to do whatever I felt was natural. That didn't go well.

When I saw him, I stood up, walked over, gave him a brief hug and peck, and said hello. Remember when I said that if I didn't say something out loud, my face sure spoke volumes for me? Yeah, that was one of those moments, and neither of us could deny it.

At one point, the kids were in school, and we just had it out. It's surprising, with all the yelling back and forth, that the new neighbors didn't call the cops. What did happen was that we realized we needed to get our shit together. We were failing miserably. We had lost ourselves as a couple, and it's easy at that point to start looking for outside attention. I never had an affair, but it sure was easy to accept a beer that a random guy would buy me when I went out with my girlfriends. I didn't realize it then, but I just wanted those sweet nothings back. I wanted back the feeling of being excited for him to come home after work. I wanted my husband back.

Arnie has a special way of making the world disappear with a hug, and there were many times I needed that. I was stronger mentally and physically, but I was a fucking shit show of a basket case because I didn't have my person. It's hard to admit to yourself that your ability to be vulnerable and patient sucks. Don't you just want to be right? Don't you just want to know that your feelings are not only valid, but true? Yeah, me too.

It took time to figure it out. At the moment of this entry, we are four years from what could have broken our family. We still have our moments of bitterness (actually, I am speaking for just me), but we attempt to fight through them. The one thing I would change about my husband is how he fights with me. He doesn't do it often, but let me tell you! He is ruthless! This man can go days without speaking one word to me unless it has to do with the kids. The silence kills me every time. I'd rather take a breath and then fight it out as soon as possible. My mind can run wild with bullshit in all the worst ways, and I become my own worst enemy.

Over the years, we have spent countless hours angry, crying, yelling, apologizing, listening, asking questions, going to therapy, and hitting Reset. There is no secret to a happy marriage. I can't give you advice on how to do anything. All I know is that, somehow, we find our way back to each other and choose each other even on the worst of days.

What I hate the most about our being mad at each other is that I can't run to him and cry, as I do with everything else. How do you confide in your best friend, ask him to hug your pain away, or ask him for advice when he's the one with whom you're fighting? I have no doubt that he was and always will be the person with whom, and for whom, I want to forever fight. I'm his pumpkin or Punky-Punky, and he's my Hunny Bunny.

Only God knows how life will work out for us, but I pray we get another seventy years together. He is still the love of my life. I feel as if God knew exactly what I needed in a person, and He made Arnie just for me. It sounds like a cliché, but forever is just too short, and writing this makes me get excited for him to come home tonight, so I can curl up to him and watch TV.

However, to keep it real, I'm sure we'll be giving each other the silent treatment, and one of us will sleep on the sofa again at some point. He'll dye my hair and paint my toes. Maybe we'll crash another wedding or pick out ridiculous outfits for each other to wear for date night. There's no telling what will happen next. Our adventure is eighteen years old and counting…

My celebrity shag is Charlie Hunnam, marry is Ryan Reynolds, and my kill would most definitely be Tom Cruise.

Chapter Six

Offspring: Pregame, Postpartum, or Hell No!

As I stated before, I knew from a very young age I wanted to be a mom. It was a hands-down, definitive life accomplishment that I knew would be nonnegotiable for me. I had always imagined this picturesque time that was going to bring love and happiness to my husband, me, and all those around us. Visions of belly rubs, foot massages, midnight cravings, ultrasound appointments, and glowing as only a pregnant woman can floated through my dreams. After baby showers were thrown and nursery decorations were hung, we would hold our tiny human in our arms with sheer bliss beaming from our bodies. Life would probably never again be as perfect as it was in that moment. That's not how it happened at all.

I became a mom for the first time at the ripe age of twenty-two. She was a complete surprise and had the most influence on who I was—as most firstborn children do. Don't get your panties in a crumble because I didn't say she was my favorite. In fact, my favorite kid changes daily; hell, it can often change hourly. What I wanted most in my life was becoming a reality whether I was ready or not.

Truth is, I was just mindlessly and obliviously walking through life before I had her. My life took a 180-degree turn when I found out I was pregnant. I had been dating this guy for a couple of years and thought things were great—or maybe I just wanted them to be. Then the fact is that I wasn't very smart when it came to birth control; I took for granted that I was having issues with my ovaries and cycles. At a young age (maybe fourteen or fifteen), I was told by a gynecologist that it would be difficult to conceive because I was diagnosed with polycystic ovary syndrome. In my fucked-up, peanut-gallery brain, that translated to not having to use birth control or condoms. I don't, for one second, regret getting pregnant because my life changed forever. I had never truly known a hard time until that very moment, nor had I known the sublime feeling of loving another human being in the purest of forms.

Before we get to the kids, let me unfold some of the twits I didn't see coming.

Whore. Slut. What the fuck were you thinking? You just want to trap me! I don't want you or this kid. Have an abortion. Kids are not to be had outside of marriage. Children of daughters you can guarantee paternity; children of sons will always bring you doubts. You need to give up your baby for adoption because you aren't married. You're a sinner. You committed adultery. What are you going to do?

Those are a few almost-verbatim comments I heard when I got pregnant. From my mother, the baby's father, his mother, the priest, and those who knew me. There was so much shame and guilt bestowed upon me that I had to celebrate quietly. I learned that pure happiness, as unexpectedly as it may come, wasn't meant to be shared with anyone.

I never had a great relationship with my mother, so how was I supposed to know how to be one. Man, she was so fucked up. She groomed me to please guys and even bought me matching bras and panties for every day of the month. I, no shit, had 30 pairs. She told me what men wanted and needed, but crucified me for being sexually active. Like, bitch, you gave me the tools and expect me not to use them? What the fuck? Looking back on it, I don't believe she was ever capable of loving me; in one way or the other, she destroyed me over the years. I also know that my earliest memory of my mother was me not liking the way she smelled; I despised her hugs. I worried that my child(ren) was going to feel the same about me. Hell, I still worry about fucking up so badly that my kids will only be left with having to walk away from me. Huge mindfuck. I spent months in a tailspin of emotions.

Then you add the guy I spent a couple of years dating. He dumped me the second I handed him the pregnancy test. Yup, this person with whom I had spent a few years, talking about marriage, kids, and life, dumped me the first chance he had. His family gave mixed reviews, to say the least. My mother called me a whore and had many other choice words for me. When I went to confess my sins, my Catholic priest told me I should give up my baby for adoption.

All that was easy, compared to seeing the look in my dad's face when I broke the news. I'm a daddy's girl through and through. The sheer disappointment was enough to leave me breathless. However, my father's love for me was deeper than his disappointment, and I will forever be grateful.

I spent the next few months dumped and dumped on. It was almost as if the pregnancy weight were as light as a feather in comparison to the words and actions of others, which felt like the weight of the world. At the time, I spoke very little to my daughter's father. Somehow, a week or so before I gave birth, he called and asked to be a part of the birth. I said yes; I wanted to give my daughter the chance to have her father in her life. I wanted her to be a daddy's girl, just as I was. I never wanted to use her against him or have her experience the pain of rejection I was feeling.

He did, in fact, show up when I called to say I was on the way to the hospital. He spent most to the time with me while I was in labor. The room I was in was filled with people I loved so dearly. They waited out my thirteen hours of labor. They made me laugh and comforted me during contractions. My loved ones moved to the hallway right outside the door when it was time to push.

Then came the sweetest moment. Their cheers filled the hallway and my room when the baby let out her first cry. The most perfect moment and the most perfect child in life was in my arms just as I had dreamed.

Hannah Sara, you have been my inspiration from the second I knew you were in my belly. You were the reason I didn't want to fail. You gave me thoughts and feelings that the most prolific of poets, the most genius of men, and the most spiritual of religions could not verbally describe. At twenty years old, you continue to impress me. You are ambitious, tenacious, and willing to help without asking. You're a girl's girl and make no excuses for it. Proud is an understatement.

So sweet, right? Well, I didn't learn shit that year. Okay, I learned a lot, but not enough to keep me from getting pregnant again. I'm a slow-ass learner, people! I need a few chances to make sure things work a certain way.

After giving birth to my beautiful, radiant little girl I tried to work things out with baby daddy. Things went exactly as you would expect. I don't like giving him much life, so I'll keep it simple. He cheated on me with several women. How did I validate my suspicions, you ask? I went to the doctor to confirm I was pregnant yet again. This time, the nurse practitioner called me back into the office a few days later. I just knew something was wrong with my baby. Nope. She called me in to tell me I had contracted chlamydia. No need to go any further.

Hannah was thirteen months old when I gave birth to a baby boy who was eight weeks premature. This pregnancy was rough, but I didn't have time to notice. I felt as if the Earth and I were spinning in opposite directions. How was I going to love another human the way I loved Hannah? How was I going to support them both on my own? How was I going to explain things to them when they got older and had questions? I had no clue.

What I did know was that this tiny little boy came into this world on a Sunday afternoon to remind me of God's love. He looked like a bitty spider, stretching his five-pound, five-ounce body as the doctor held him so that I could see him for the first time. His cry was soft, and he exuded tender peace. I don't know how to explain what I felt the moment I held him.

Antonio Samuel, your kindness has been felt since the moment I held you. Your quiet presence fills rooms and hearts. Your laugh is as silly as your sense of humor. I adore your bright light and how you make me want to be a better person. Your dance moves have gone from two left feet to one and a half, but your singing is ten out of ten. You're going to do something great in life and will enrich the lives you touch. I love you forever and always, my son.

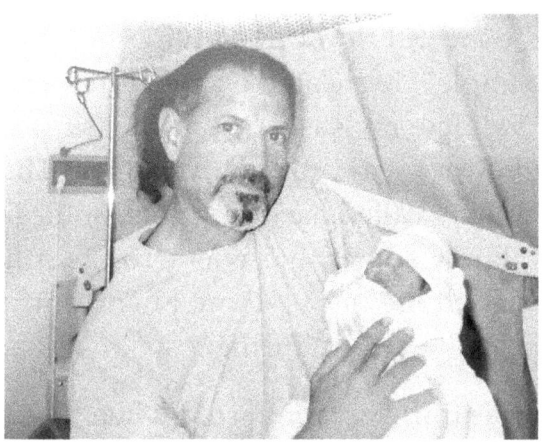

By this time, I had seen the light! There I was, twenty-three years old, two babies, working two (sometimes three) jobs, and very lost. I think being anorexic in high school was a test drive for being a single mom. Money was so tight that there were days I didn't eat to ensure the babies had what they needed. I once shared a bag of popcorn because that's all we had to eat because I wasn't going to get paid until the following day. My family was going through the roughest times I had ever seen. It was the beginning of some things, and the beginning of the end for others.

I met my husband when Hannah was nineteen months old, and Samuel was eight months old. My oldest memory of Arnie with Hannah was the first time we took her on a date with us. She was the cutest little thing running around the city of Austin! As the day ended, we took her to eat at McDonald's and let her go outside to play shortly after she finished. Arnie was not only patient and kind all day, but he also played with her on the slide. They ran around the playground as if they had known each other her whole life. Never had I seen a man play with a child like that. Hannah would randomly ask for Arnie when he returned to his duty station, and it made me feel as if this could really work. We had agreed that I would stay home to raise the kids. We had similar ideas about what family meant to us, and how raising our children would come second to nothing. How we would end up actually doing it was a different story.

In early September 2004, I became pregnant with my third baby—my husband's first. We were both over-the-moon excited as we purposefully worked at it. I remember calling my dad to let him know, and the only thing he asked was if I would be getting married. I giggled and told him I promised I would; Arnie wasn't going anywhere. Now, we all have to remember that I had previously been dumped… twice…and to add insult to injury, my father still hadn't met Arnie. Yeah, I know.

The months rolled on, and we did, in fact, get married while enjoying that season of life. On December 8, I woke up not feeling well. My belly and lower back ached. Arnie and I decided that I'd probably slept wrong, so we went to the mall to walk around to see if it would help. A few hours later, the pain became more intense, however still bearable. That evening, Arnie took me to the emergency room, where the doctor ordered an ultrasound. We got to see our baby for the first and last time. I'm not sure why, but I've always referred to the baby as a girl. As we watched her on the screen, we saw her heart stop beating. It was there. Then there was nothing.

My heart sank with hers. We would never get to hold her. We would never get to name her. We would never get to enjoy her personality. We would never hear her giggle or play with her siblings. I was approximately fourteen weeks along when I miscarried her. She would be seventeen pushing eighteen this summer. Our family still talks about her and wonders what life would have been like with her. One day, I'll get to see our sweet angel.

Months passed, and life only lent itself to a CliffsNotes style of the grieving process. July of 2005, we found out we were pregnant once more. Although I was thrilled and excited, I couldn't help but worry. On top of being the pregnant mom of a two-year-old and a twenty-month-old, Arnie was getting deployed for a year. That idea alone was overwhelming.

Arnie deployed in September, and I had my first ultrasound a few weeks later. While I was anticipating a gender reveal during the anatomy scan of our baby, I wasn't prepared for seeing what I thought was his umbilical cord. The ultrasound tech was very professional, and as he kindly showed me pictures of my baby, he joined in my excitement that it was a baby boy. Once he was done printing pictures, he asked me to wait in the waiting room because the doctor would like to follow up with me. Now, I hadn't had a ton of kids or ultrasounds, but I knew this wasn't going well.

The doctor was in surgery, and I had to wait until he made it out of the surgical unit. I called my daddy to voice my concerns and for him to calm me as only he can. When the doctor finally appeared, I was sitting on a hospital bed in the recovery room. This man wearing green scrubs sat next to me to tell me our son would be born with gastroschisis. He explained that gastroschisis is a congenital birth defect in which the baby's abdomen doesn't fully close and that his intestines would be out of his belly when he was born. I never voiced it at the time, but I knew exactly what that was because I had a friend whose child was born the same way and had grown to be a wonderfully healthy adult. I smiled at the doctor and told him I knew everything would be okay with my baby. He looked at me and asked if I understood what he was telling me. I confirmed and repeated that my baby would be just fine.

Within a week, I started seeing a specialist in Nashville for all my obstetrics and prenatal care. Twice a week, I checked on our little nugget, once for me and once for him. Things got complicated when my body started having contractions and dilating months before I was due. Ama came to stay with me to help out, but my body just wasn't having it. The doctor requested Arnie come home from Iraq to help. I picked him up the day before Thanksgiving and then was on bed rest as much as possible.

At one of the baby's appointments, we were told the hole in his abdomen was starting to close. That would have been the best news ever if the closing tissue had not begun cutting off circulation to the intestine.

Two months before I was due, I wasn't feeling well. By that same evening, I had a fever. We rushed to the emergency room in Nashville, knowing things were about to get even more complicated. After having an amniocentesis, the doctors told us I had an infection in my amniotic sac. As this was being told to us, there were so many doctors and nurses pulling, tugging, poking, and prepping me for an emergency C-section. I was signing papers that I didn't understand, and I was scared out of my mind.

When they rolled me out of the room I was in, I remember being so anxious and overwhelmed that I let out a yell. I couldn't control the shaking or the yell. Any woman who's experienced an emergency C-section knows what I'm talking about. The stark, cold room, the bright light in your face, and the people talking around you, but you can't quite understand what anyone is saying. Thankfully, my husband was finally allowed in the room to hold my hand.

At just past nine thirty in the morning on a cold January day, our son was born. Arnie said he was blue because the umbilical cord was wrapped around his neck, and his intestine just hung from his belly as they quickly transferred him to a table to get him to breathe. After he let out his first cry, I couldn't stop crying. He made it! A nurse wrapped him in a blanket and showed him to me from afar. I didn't get to smell him, snuggle him with my cheek, or even give him a kiss before they took him away. Arnie left with him as the doctors finished with me.

At some point that evening, Arnie came back to me with a picture of our son. He had already had his first corrective surgery to save his life, and his daddy wasn't going to be anywhere but with him. Michael Andrew came eight weeks early, weighed six pounds, fourteen ounces, and fought harder than any heavyweight champion I've ever seen. Arnie spent his time going back and forth between us in the hospital because I wasn't allowed to see Michael Andrew for three days after he was born. I think it was because I had to finish the antibiotics I was on to ensure I wouldn't infect him.

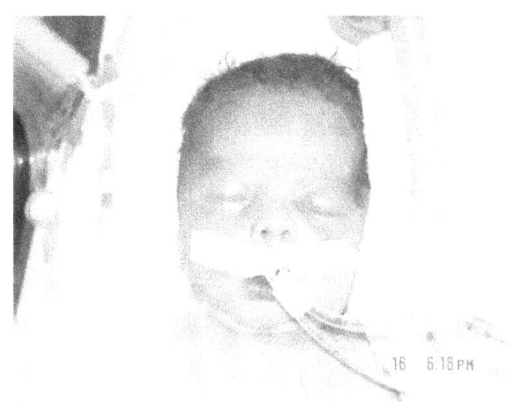

Our warrior. Our fighter. Our gift from God. Michael faced two additional surgeries, as part of his intestine had died. We also found out he was born with Wolff-Parkinson-White syndrome (WPW) and auditory neuropathy. In all, he spent a couple of months in the NICU, but he overcame all the setbacks. In March of 2022, he underwent a heart ablation to correct the WPW.

Michael, your laugh is infectious. You love and accept people in the purest of forms. Determination is your middle name, and failure is nowhere in your vocabulary. God showed us grace, love, mercy, and perfection when He made you. Anyone in your path is lucky to have you in their lives. I'm not sure what life will bring, but I do know you'll embrace it with your infectious smile and laughter. I love you with everything in me, *papito*.

Whew! Reminiscing about our little angel and Michael has me feeling all the things! Break time. I need to compose myself because there's a lot more to this chapter.

I'm back, and we are picking up a year later when Arnie left to go to yet another Army school called Basic Noncommissioned Officer Course (BNOC). He came home to visit one weekend. There's nothing special or fancy about this visit, except for finding out a few weeks later that we had made another baby. Let me tell you, Arnie was fucking pissed when I told him! Ha! He told me it was impossible for me to be pregnant; I think, for a second, he forgot how babies were made.

After confirming our new pregnancy, we made the best of it. Come to find out, Arnie wasn't pissed at all. He was scared. He had a right to be scared. I had already had two premature babies, a miscarriage, and our son was still being followed by several specialists. His perspective was real and raw. I had always taken a different view, but I couldn't take away his pain or hesitation.

During my now fifth pregnancy, Arnie deployed yet again. This time, it would be a year in Afghanistan. Due to our previous experience, he sent me to live with my mother. I know; I hated it as well. Things weren't as bad then as they would eventually get, so whatever. The greatest thing about spending that much time in Austin was that I was back with Ama. She calls Samuel her roommate and Michael her boyfriend. The four of us were inseparable. Hannah started prekinder that August, so the boys and I ran errands and hit every thrift store we could with Ama before picking her up after school.

I was monitored closely by a high-risk OB/GYN and eventually started weekly progesterone injections to keep the fetus viable. Aside from eating everything I could and craving Bloody Marys (which I curbed by drinking a ton of V8), things were going very well. Baby was growing and healthy. Each scan showed perfection, and I was having the time of my life.

On a beautiful December Monday, Katherine Elaine joined our family. I was on the phone with Arnie when the doctor came in to check my progress. She told us to get ready because we were about to start pushing. Arnie may have been thousands of miles away, but we had our baby via teleconference, and he got to cheer me on and hear her first cry. She was this perfectly round baby with a head full of hair. It didn't take her long to open her eyes to see the world she would be taking on.

Katherine, your intelligence is unmatched. You see the world as an object to be explored. You're inquisitive, thoughtful, direct, and a complete hoot. You never cease to amaze or shock us with your ball-busting jokes. I'm not sure what the future holds for you, but I do know that if you don't like it, you'll do something about it. Keep exploring and asking questions, kid. You're cool AF, and I love you to pieces.

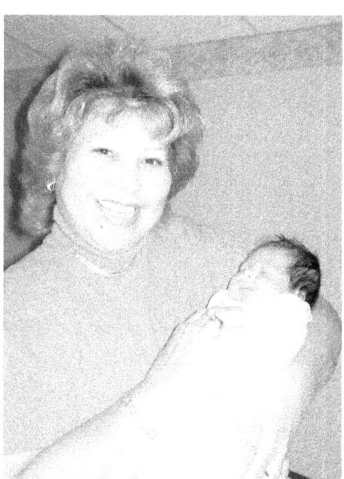

During my pregnancy with Katherine, Arnie brought up the conversation about getting my tubes tied. I wasn't ready to give up that part of my life. I understood that my body wasn't doing so well with pregnancy, and he could have lost me while having Michael. My heart wasn't vibing with his pragmatism. After discussing it several times with him and my doctor, I decided to go through with it. Three hours after giving birth, the doctor tied my tubes.

Three months later, Arnie came home for two weeks and finally met his baby girl. We spent those weeks traveling to see friends and family. We even changed our surprise couples' trip Arnie had planned for me; instead of Hawaii, we went to Disney World. Welcome to parenthood. Things were great, but short-lived, as he had to return to Afghanistan.

The five of us made our way back to Tennessee, where we celebrated Arnie's return. Life progressed, but something just wasn't right. Come to find out, I had postpartum depression. I struggled to do the most basic of chores. I cried all the time. Arnie and I fought more than usual. The worst part was that I was no longer enjoying what I loved the most—my children. After seeing a doctor, he gave me a ton of medication. If I remember correctly, I was taking seven different prescriptions twice a day. My body was taking a hit, and my mind was giving up.

Instead of giving up, at my request, Arnie checked me into a psychiatric hospital in Nashville. I was only there a week, if I'm not mistaken, but it made a difference. Meds were changed, I slept, and I talked to people who were struggling just as I was, if not worse.

When I got home and saw our kids, I knew I would forever do what I needed to stay with them. That's when the hard part started. I went cold turkey and stopped taking all the medications I had been on for months.

Please **DO NOT** *change or stop taking medication(s) without consulting with your doctor.*

The withdrawals were intense. Arnie didn't understand what I was going through. The kids were just kids needing and wanting kid things. Arnie's job was demanding. My mother had fucked up in Austin, and we moved her in with us, just for her to tell Arnie I was worthless. No, really. There were many conversations she attempted to have with Arnie over the years, telling him he deserved someone better. That he should leave me and find someone worth his time.

Maybe I didn't have postpartum depression. Maybe I had a very hectic life, needed sleep, and not to be put down by my own mother. It didn't matter how much I loved my husband, kids, or even my mother. Things fucking sucked! I hated myself. All of me. You should have seen how ugly I was. My hair, my wire-framed glasses, and my body were just as distorted as my mind. I was drowning while still breathing. My heart hurt so much, and I can still feel the pain as I type this. The tears don't come down as they once did, but my forty-two-year-old self wants to hug my twenty-eight-year-old self.

My mother's antics hadn't worked to separate my husband and me, so I guess that's when she upped the ante. One week prior to her going full-on slut, psycho bitch, I had a uterine ablation because my periods were so heavy and lasting weeks at a time. Y'all, I was exhausted in every way imaginable.

To follow the disaster that had become my life, I became paralyzed with fear of motherhood. Although I had met a couple of women whom I admired from afar, I didn't have a good example of what a mother should be. This daughter who was lost for so many years became a mom to do…what? Fuck up her kids too? Was I able to love my kids? Teach them? Did they cringe when I held them, the way I once did with my mother? Did they trust me? Hell, did I trust myself? Nothing felt right. It made me terribly sad that I had everything I had ever wanted, and I couldn't enjoy it.

After all hell broke loose with my mother and I kicked her out, I needed to find myself. I needed to heal. I had no idea how or what that meant.

You know what life did give me? Yup, another pregnancy. This time, there was no test to pee on or doctor's appointment to confirm. We had gone to walk around a hardware store after dinner one night. I told Arnie that I felt pregnant. Mind you, I had already had my tubes tied and a uterine ablation. This should have been impossible. Arnie looked at me as if I was crazy but went along with it.

A few days later, I went to work; I was a receptionist at an imaging center. I was cramping and not feeling so great. I asked the ultrasound tech to scan me to see if I had a ruptured ovarian cyst—at least that's what I told her. She started the scan and quickly asked if I was pregnant. She showed me what looked like two little bubbles on the screen and said it was twins. She also informed me the pregnancy wouldn't be viable.

This wasn't what I wanted. I wanted to be pregnant again, even if it was against all odds. That wasn't God's plan. I knew that *if* I was indeed pregnant, it wouldn't last long. I was thankful for the moment, even if it only lasted for the week that I had my suspicions.

Miscarrying this time wasn't as difficult to endure. It was a lot like a period. Some cramping, bleeding, and then life went on. Except, I didn't really stop bleeding this time. From January 2002 to September 2002, I had a period that lasted three weeks out of every month. The ablation should have solved all issues for three to five years, but my periods became so heavy that I often had golf-ball-sized clots and had to wear a tampon and pad at the same time. Even so, I would drench them in an hour.

I went in on a Thursday to see the gynecologist, and by the following Tuesday, I was having a hysterectomy. I cried for days leading up to the surgery. As much as my body was going through, I was still hardheaded and didn't want to let go of what I thought motherhood and womanhood meant. Arnie took me to the hospital and held me as I was getting prepped for surgery. As I cried, he reminded me how much he and our kids needed me. How I was more than a pregnant woman. Five and a half hours later, parts of my body that had given me the most beautiful children and memories were gone. Ten days post-op, Arnie left for Afghanistan again. I'm telling you, the Army doesn't give one fuck! LOL.

In all seriousness, please know that I am fully aware there are women out there who have faced so much worse. My heart hurts for them—for you. This is just my story and how it's unfolded. I am also fully aware of how incredibly blessed and lucky I am to have our four kids and three angels waiting for us in heaven. I, by no means, want to diminish the life and experience of another woman. I also don't expect anyone to feel sorry for me. I tell this for us all. To know that pain and joy often come in tandem. I'm ten years past the hysterectomy, and now I'm super thankful for it.

Hannah is now twenty and is still all things girly. She is so silly! There hasn't been a time in her life that she hasn't been dancing or trying to look pretty. This child had every princess doll with the matching prince. I mean, how can a princess not have a prince, right? She pranced around in her princess dresses with the matching tiara and heels. It was a daily sound for her to be clacking around the house, pushing a baby stroller.

Hannah spends her days annoying her dad by taking his sweatshirts, eating his ice cream, or stealing his lotion. She is the most hyper of all the kids and laughs at her own jokes (just like her mom). I'm most proud of how she reflects on herself to enhance or change her behavior. She listens to others with a tender heart, but can tell you how she feels in a second. Her attitude has been one hell of a ride! I think amusement parks get ideas for roller coasters from the teenage eye roll. Those things are intense!

I will say that the years between ten and fourteen were the hardest. She made us parents, so we learn with her. My husband and I *attempt* to take the time while parenting her to remind ourselves of what we were doing at her age and, most importantly, what we needed at that age. This helps us understand her better. I mean, it truly has become our go-to for all our kids since they are all so different.

Hannah has a special way of being my saving grace when the other kids are driving me batshit crazy. I love our talks, our movie binges, and how she still wants me to hold her. She randomly fills my gas tank, buys me special soap she finds on clearance to help with my eczema, and lays a blanket over her daddy when he falls asleep on the sofa. She's the keeper of secrets for her siblings and the coordinator of surprise birthday parties.

She's in college, works, and is learning to be independent. Her dreams are all over the place, and she often finds herself frustrated because of it. We reassure her that this is the time for her to explore the world. There is no need for her to have all the answers (none of us will ever have all the answers).

Right now is the time for her to learn who she is, who she wants to be, and to fuck up as she's doing so. But, most of all, today will always be a great day to celebrate who she's become.

Samuel is nineteen, stubborn, and goofy as fuck! Picture this: I'm going into labor for what seemed like the twentieth time in one week, and I'm eight weeks early. They pull this baby boy from my womb, and all I can think about is how ugly he is!! The doctor holds him up just as Rafiki held Simba, and I cringe as if it were one of those crazed hyenas instead. Lord, I thought they switched my baby! So I did what any normal, sane person would do and took a deep breath. I said to myself, *Mindy Jo, this is your baby boy, and he is special, girl!* Turns out, this baby was even more special than what I described earlier.

Y'all, he had a heart of gold, and it's still the same! He's compassionate, kind, and generous. He has a thug-ish side (or so he thinks). He loves trap music, cusses as if he's auditioning to be Samuel L. Jackson's sidekick, and picks an argument just for fun. Our student-athlete with great grades was SUSPENDED from school for slapboxing with another boy in the middle school bathroom. Hell, I didn't even know what slapboxing meant. I remember getting the call from the assistant principal. I knew there had to be a mistake. Not Samuel. Michael, yes. Katherine, sure. Samuel? NO! Then I heard his voice in the background. Yup, Samuel. He was pleased with himself because the other kid never landed a punch. Jeez. He's the most multifaceted child we have.

Samuel has big dreams of becoming a pediatrician. So far, he's worked to achieve that dream. One day at a time, one study guide at a time, one piece of knowledge at a time. His brain can be chaotic, forgetful, and he has hyperactive tendencies that complicate his days, but he never gives up.

Michael is seventeen, balls-to-the-wall, and athletic. The child has been nonstop since he learned to walk. Due to being moderately to severely deaf, he understands the world around him in ways I never knew. He also has a learning disability, which makes it a little more difficult for him to be a typical seventeen-year-old. Nothing he's gone through has ever made him give up. Michael is a fighter, a lover, and incredibly hardworking.

He has strong tactile skills, and when put to use, can build the best of fences, decks, and other things using wood. He is mechanically inclined. He changes the oil in our cars. He's helped replace brakes and taillights. Michael also has strong discipline. You'll catch him up and out of the house at six o'clock on a weekend morning to get in an extra run. The challenge to beat his current-max bench press keeps him in the garage working out. Drive, determination, and persistence is everything he is made of.

This kid is also our jokester. There's never any telling what he and Hannah will be getting into when they get together. They are the buddy team that never stops laughing, talking shit, and making Target/Starbucks runs thirty minutes before they close. They are quite the duo.

Katherine is fifteen; she broke the mold and keeps us on our toes. I'm not entirely sure where she gets her ideas or sense of humor, but I'm often left speechless. She has a high IQ and a low tolerance for bullshit. She's guarded, introverted, and monotone. However, when she's ready to be outgoing and silly, Katherine can be the life of a party. Not in a dancing-queen way, but in a way that'll make you laugh until your belly hurts.

She sends me down rabbit holes with brainy hypotheses that I normally don't fully understand. Out of all the kids, she spends the most time with me. She cuddles at night with me at least two to three times a week. For years, we have asked each other three questions while lying in the dark. Everything from our favorite colors to what we hate the most in life.

Samuel and Katherine make up the other buddy team that we affectionately dubbed Pinky and the Brain. You should know why if you've ever watched the cartoon. One is just as inquisitive as the other. They have a very special bond that consists of anime, video games, and dark humor.

Our family stays busy, which helps me enjoy when we can hide out at home. The kids are always doing something that is either entertaining or driving me batshit crazy! I thought taking care of four kids under five was difficult until we got to this stage. Now it's fighting over social media, dances, boyfriends, girlfriends, belly-button piercings, and tattoos. It's just never-ending.

There is nothing that we won't discuss with our kids; our approach is to catch them before someone else gets to them. I'm not going to lie and say that I'm always calm and composed during our conversations. Most often, I'm Googling terms in the Urban Dictionary, calling Kelley, crying to my dad, or squeezing my husband's hand. There is no rule book, so here goes everything! Nothing in the world can move me like the four of them. On the other hand, these fools are the reason I drink. Cheers to my little liver!

Arnie and I have found that listening to them and then asking questions works to our advantage. Talking at the kids or trying to stuff them with how-tos, rules, and expectations always fails and ends up turning them away from us. When we listen, they speak. When we stay calm, they learn to trust the process of communication. When we question them, it gives them the opportunity to think, process, and understand themselves.

We aren't trying to raise followers. It's imperative to be open and honest about our lives so that our kids will learn how to make choices and lead their own lives. The older they get, the more information we share.

The other aspect to our parenting—the hardest part, in fact—is the tough love. From a very young age, we have reinforced the concepts of rewards and consequences. Each choice in life has a path. The right thing isn't always the easiest or most fun, but you'll have to live with yourself, one way or the other. You might as well look in the mirror and be proud of yourself.

I want to close this chapter with this: Regardless of what role kids play in your life—and even if you decide not to have children—it's okay. You're right in how you feel—excitement, despair, fear, love, hate, disappointment, hope, or anything else. It took me a long time to know that I am not my mother, I have the power within me to change the past, to make a better today for our kids. Most importantly, I will continue to learn from our kids as I see the world through their eyes.

Hannah, Samuel, Michael, and Katherine…each of you are truly amazing, and I'm beyond thankful to God that I get to be your mama.

Chapter Seven

Sex: The Forbidden Fruit or Let's Play!

***W**ARNING! The beginning of this chapter may be triggering. Please skip it if you must, and seek help if this triggers any traumatic experience.*

Religion, culture, health, word of mouth, molestation, rape, sexual harassment, sex trafficking, drugs, alcohol, and so many other things can and will affect your perception of sex, regardless of age. I was molested at the age of seven, and things didn't get better. The first time it happened scared me to my core. I didn't know what or how or why; I just knew this was not okay. As in many cases, it was a family friend, and there was no escaping this person because I didn't tell anyone.

Shame, disgust, confusion, self-loathing, and fear were a few feelings that stayed with me for decades to come. Unfortunately, this wasn't an isolated incident. The molestation continued, not only by the family friend, but also by a family member. That took a couple of years to end. It was infrequent, as we didn't see each other but a couple of times a year, but it never got easier—the anxiety, the trying to hide and avoid them, the everything. I remember telling them that I didn't like what they were doing and that I didn't want to be around them. It didn't deter them. They threatened to tell my mother it was my idea; that was their way of controlling me and the situation. I already knew how much my mother didn't like me. This would just escalate her hatred for me—at least that was my perception.

Years later, I found out that I was right. I was in my late twenties when I finally said something to my mother. Her exact response was, "You don't expect me to stop talking to my family just because of this, right?" I told her I didn't expect anything and only said something to her because she asked why I was so depressed. At the time, there were so many things going on with me, and I had never healed from the sexual trauma, which added to the already mounting issues.

During the important years of self-discovery and social growth, I learned how lost I truly was. Middle school became my theatrical stage, the place I flexed my talents. You know, the smile that didn't fade, filling every waking second of the day, and trying to perfect the lying, cheating, and stealing in order to cover the disgusting person I was. Little did I know that it was only making my life all the more difficult.

In sixth grade, things were not going so well. Chaos was my middle name, and, boy, was my mother having a rough time with me. There was a point at which she started taking her lunch break at the same time I had mine so that she could pick me up, take me home, and spank me. If I was late to class, I went home. If I got a low grade, I went home. If I was talking too much in class, I went home. I giggle at it now, but back then I had to come up with more lies to explain why my face was red and swollen when my mother drove me back to school after the spankings. I had to come up with excuses that didn't further embarrass me.

To exaggerate my insulting behavior, I stole a ring from a girl's house the one and only time I was invited to spend the night. I didn't steal it because it was expensive or because I needed it. I stole it thinking, if I had something of hers, maybe I could be like her. I could be happy…and pretty…and have friends. The sexual trauma I had endured caused more problems for me than just insecurities. I didn't know how to be a decent human. I fucked over people who never deserved it, just because I was hiding and losing myself.

Some may wonder how sexual trauma can affect someone's life in these ways. Well, my answer is I don't know. All I do know is how incredibly lonely and vile I felt. I was willing to do or say anything to be accepted, even for a brief moment. Those brief moments, though, came with a price tag.

I became consensually sexually active at the age of sixteen. Things were different with him. He was kind, patient, and gentle with my heart. It was the first time I knew safety, even if I unknowingly fought it. We never became wildly active or adventurous in our endeavors. Looking back at our time together, I now know he was just what I needed. Surely, the same cannot be said in return; however, I am thankful for the safe transitional period he offered.

Then came the second guy I dated. If "will not come" were a person, this bitch would be the poster child. I didn't know then how selfish he truly was. It was on his time, how he wanted, and it was over when he was done. I hope the women after me had better luck.

I've messed around with guys in between who were nothing spectacular, or even mediocre. I was always left wondering if I was doing something wrong because I was not experiencing the shit my girlfriends were talking about.

Now, one guy stands out simply because he was fun and gave me a lot of attention. Maybe not the cutest, but he most definitely brought lots of laughs. I had to find a way to end things nicely because I knew he wanted more than I could have ever given him. How did I do that? I went back to my ex-boyfriend and got pregnant. I'm a real winner, y'all!

Backtracking a couple of years, I was raped by a guy I knew. It was a typical Lifetime movie. Party girl goes out, gets drunk, gets into a friendly vehicle, gets raped, says nothing, and small-town bullshit friendliness continues. To be fair, I never thought I had been raped until my therapist taught me the different types of rape. I may not have had all the same feelings as I did when I was seven, and then ten to twelve, but the embarrassment, anxiety, and worthlessness was written all over me, even if no one else could see it but me.

As I rolled into my (God willing) final relationship, I knew sex was overrated and lots of trouble. I told my would-be husband that sex was off the table when he asked me to be his girlfriend. This was greeted with kindness and acceptance. After two weeks of long, late night conversations, he came home for his brother's wedding, and as life and hormones would have it, things took a turn. No need to repeat what I already said about our first time. I will say that it was the start of a healing journey that I have been on for more than eighteen years.

Something I wasn't expecting to feel was how uncomfortable it was at times to breastfeed. My past sexual trauma crept into the present and tainted moments that were meant for the wonders of human biology to work its magic as I breastfed my children and bonded with them. There were times I cringed when my kids hugged me or accidentally brushed against my breast. I still feel overstimulated at times; occasionally it sends eerie vibrations throughout me when my husband holds my hand and rubs it with his thumb. No joke, I literally stabbed someone in the ear with a pen because they came up behind me and scared the fuck out of me!

The other things that have shaped my view on sex are religion and culture. Both told me to wait until marriage to have sex. Both said you had to be an obedient, good girl. Both shamed sexual confidences. Both have stark double standards.

But what did all that mean? I was already a bad girl because someone had touched me. Who fucking cared if I didn't want or ask for it? I was already damaged goods before I even knew what sex was. So, again, who fucking cared if was I a virgin or not? I was a sinner a thousandfold over before I knew what that even meant. So who fucking cared that I was chugging wine at the age of thirteen while prepping for Holy Communion before 7:30 a.m. Catholic Mass as an altar server?

Nothing in my life made sense. I was drowning in lies, and the nightmares sucked. I knew, somehow, I needed to pull myself out of the hellhole I was in. That's when I started telling my husband my story, little by little. Arnie became even more gentle with me with each conversation. And not only sexually, but emotionally. He became my safe space.

He was the first and only man with whom I have ever made love. Like real love. That intimate part of sex that touches your soul and binds you to another human, like none before or anything imaginable. This wasn't just kissing. This was a connection. This wasn't just penetration. This was becoming one. Arnie is forever my Garden of Eden, my perfection, my love.

As time moved forward and safety was discovered, we were able to discover a whole new life together. Fun, exciting, sensual, passionate, adventurous, fulfilling, lustful, playful, and arousing are some of the words I now use to describe sex. What was once obligation and dirty has now become so damn wonderful!

I never understood why women talked about getting cranky when they didn't have sex. Now I do. There have been times in our marriage that we have had sex four times in one day and at least once a day for days on end. Then there are times that a dry spell comes along and lasts a couple of weeks. Nothing is wrong; we are just busy and exhausted at the end of the day.

Morning sex is one of my faves. I think foreplay throughout the day makes things exciting. We have even had fun making up new roles for ourselves.

Once, we spent the weekend alone in Nashville and were down on Broadway and Second Avenue having a grand ole time. Arnie went to the bathroom and returned as a stranger. Of course, I played along, and things got a little out of hand. Arnie, as the stranger, hit on me. I stuck to the story that my husband went to the bathroom and hadn't returned. The stranger tells me I'm too beautiful to be left alone for that long; he has a nice hotel room in which he can keep me company. I agree to leave with the stranger.

We get into a cab and continue our charade. As I continue giggling, I make ridiculous comments about how mad my husband will be when he finds out I left with some strange man. The strange man caresses my crossed leg while softly kissing me, ignoring anything I have to say. Our cabdriver slips a peek in the rearview mirror every now and then. We arrive at the hotel moments later. The stranger helps me out of the car and slips a nice tip to the driver.

As I take in our new surroundings, the stranger grabs me by the hand, pulls me in, and kisses me as we wait for the elevator. Gushing over him and his stealth-like moves, he tells me there's more fun to be had. We enter the glass elevator with another couple. As sly as they try to be, I see them peeking at the stranger and whore wife that left her husband in a bar bathroom. The stranger gently pushes me up against the glass and kisses me again. As the elevator door opens, he takes my hand and walks me to his room. I walk in thinking only the unimaginable will happen next, and it did. We fell on the bed…laughing our asses off!

I'm in shambles thinking of this night! Yes, we had sex, but that was just sex. We laughed so hard that night and the following morning. Hell, we are *still* laughing at the cabdriver and the other couple. It's stupid fun that can only be had between us, and that alone makes it special.

We have also given each other the nicknames of Paul and Paulina. The running joke comes from Paul Revere and the Minutemen. I'm not a historian, so I don't even know if the band's name even makes sense, but it's self-explanatory when women joke about men coming too quickly. Arnie and I perfected the quickie after years of exploration to ensure we both left satisfied. Y'all, we have four kids, so you have to get it in when you can. Hell, we went on a couples' trip with some of my absolute favorite people and had to put this technique into use then too.

We have also been walked in on by our kids. Never a fun time, but those fuckers now know how to knock *and* not to pick the lock. Yes, we have had to add an extra lock to our bedroom door. There was also this one time that the youngest was still sleeping in bed with us. She must have been about eighteen months old or so, and we thought she was asleep.

We tried to do the deed and thought we were doing well by not making any noise or moving around too much. Hell no! She didn't move or even fully wake up, but in her sleepy little baby voice, she told us to stop dancing. That is another one of those memories that still makes us laugh.

We've never been into toys. The touching, kissing, and all the stuff that goes with it has always proven to be more than effective. Then my forty-second birthday came around. One of my very good friends knew I had never owned a vibrator and corrected that issue by gifting me one. I laughed so hard when I opened my gift. I will say it took about a month before I gave it a test drive. Um, all I can say is that I went too long without this beautiful pink contraption. Everyone deserves a friend like her.

My introduction to sex wasn't pleasant. I don't wish my experience on anyone, much less anything worse. What I do wish for everyone is healing, self-love, and a feeling of safety. I learned that what happened to me wasn't my fault. That I wasn't just that dirty, bad girl who made piss-poor choices. That I am worth not only glorious and fulfilling sex, but *respect*. My body has changed over the years, and I've gained fifty-five pounds since meeting my husband, but that doesn't negate my beauty or what I have to offer my husband. Having a hysterectomy didn't make me less of a woman. In all actuality, it made things so much better.

Another aspect of my healing journey was raising our kids. It was a twofold blessing. First, the greatest gift Arnie ever gave me was being able to stay home to raise our kids. This was deliberate. We knew we didn't want outside influences on our kids until they were old enough to tell us about their day. From a very early age, I told the kids that their bodies were private. I named specific people who were allowed to change their diapers or give them baths. You may find it odd to start telling your kids these things at such a young age, but the fact was that I wasn't willing to take a chance with our children's safety. I would rather it be one of their earliest memories than for them not to tell me something inappropriate happened.

The second part is my ongoing communication with the children, except the conversations have obviously evolved. We have two girls and two boys. I would say about ninety-nine percent of the conversations are the same. What we expect out of our boys, we expect out of our girls' boyfriends, and vice versa. Respect goes both ways. *No means no!* Then there are times that yes means no. For instance, if your date gets drunk, and she wants to have sex. Don't do it. Leave her alone, and let her sleep it off. You are not free to act stupidly just because you find someone who's attractive or who's garnered a less than desirable reputation. Respect all girls and women as you would your mother or sisters, regardless of how a female is dressed or acting. Kissing and telling is for slimy little bitches; don't do it.

For our daughters, you don't owe anyone anything. *Period.* Money in any form does not translate to owning or owing. You are allowed to set the tempo. Time does not lead to physical touch of any sort. Dress to impress only yourself. Watch how he treats the women in his life (and you), and you'll get a sneak peek of what's to come. Respect does not expire or correspond to age.

These are just a few things we emphasize to our kids. The conversations and expectations go both ways. We have them as a group of six, one-on-one, or one of the kids will pull both of us aside for private and personal advice. This chapter shouldn't have had anything to do with kids, but the intricacies are so important, and it would be irresponsible for us to not have these conversations with them.

What has formed your perspective on sex? How has it evolved over time? Do you want more or less of it? Have you ever felt constricted by society or even your own personal thoughts? Can a woman truly feel free to explore her sexuality without it being tied to some type of trauma? What conversations have you had with yourself, your partner, and your children?

I still have moments of self-hatred, and probably always will, but with the love I have found (with my husband and, most importantly, within myself), the healing I have worked toward, and the faith I have in God, I will also forever combat those thoughts and feelings. I will forever hold on to the special moments in time that have brought so much to me.

In short, at the ripe old age of forty-two, I'm a "let's play" kinda gal.

Chapter Eight

Shopping: Brand Whore or Red-Tag Diva

A girl should be two things: classy and fabulous.
—Coco Chanel

With that said, I'm classy and fabulous on a tight budget. Maybe not so much classy or fabulous, but tight budget is a great description. I grew up having the wants. The needs were always hanging in the balance. My brother and I had a swing set, a Game Boy was gifted to us from Santa, yearly we went back-to-school shopping, and we ate out almost daily. Wants. The needs, like electricity and water, were always a surprise. I'm not going to blame one parent over the other, but paying bills just wasn't a top priority; at least, that's how it seemed. Every once in a while, the water was cut off as someone (usually my daddy) was showering because the bill didn't get paid. Same would happen with the electricity.

Let me say that I don't think this happened intentionally. My parents had such a tumultuous relationship that, looking back, I'm surprised this didn't happen more often. My father loved his toys. His bass boat and fishing rods, any and all guns, hunting trips, and then he bought a Harley-Davidson. Gorgeous, fun, badass, and expensive. The weekend bike runs, accessories, and eclectic friends made this absolutely appealing to me.

Daddy worked very hard and played the same. He was a firefighter, and later became an EMT. This was before these jobs became joined at the hip. Daddy worked twenty-four hours on and forty-eight hours off as a firefighter; then he changed clothes to work twelve-hour shifts as an EMT. We lived in Del Rio, Texas, which was two and a half hours from the nearest city. There were nights he would get called in at 2:00 a.m. to urgently help drive a patient to a hospital capable of caring for critical patients. Again, very hard worker.

Mother worked at a furniture store as a sales lady. She later changed jobs, and by the time she left us, she had gone through a few clerical and secretarial positions. She filled her time off with cleaning and going to church. I don't remember her having friends with which she lunched or had girls' nights. Where Daddy was outgoing and busy, Mother was a loner, and I guess she entertained herself. I think she tried keeping up with Daddy, but you could tell she just wasn't happy. She was very involved with our local Catholic church and helped in any way she could. She used to cook a roaster full of chili to make Frito-and-chili bags; she sold them at the yearly jamboree to raise money for the church. Daddy helped her transport her items and set things up. She was also very involved with the youth group, which made my involvement mandatory.

Daddy took us out on his boat, and the faster he ran that bitch, the bigger the smile on my face. Mother wasn't impressed and always worried something bad would happen. When Daddy entered bass tournaments, Mother went to a family friend's house to prepare for a large-scale fish fry. When Daddy went out for the day on his motorcycle, Mother stayed home. I, on the other hand, couldn't wait to get on that bike. Some of my favorite memories with Daddy were going with him on poker runs and competing in races, like the pickle bite, at bike rallies.

"Different" doesn't fully explain just how opposite my mother and father sat on any spectrum, so it was no surprise that money wasn't really discussed. It's easy to look back and see how easy it was for communication to be almost nonexistent, which complicated everything. Don't take this as me talking shit about my parents. These are just examples of how things, including money, can disintegrate when the left hand doesn't talk to the right hand. As a matter of fact, my husband and I have found ourselves in these situations, especially after a deployment. He tries to pay bills, I try to pay bills, he forgets one, I think he paid it, and vice versa; then there's a disconnection notice in the mail. Shit happens; then we pay it.

My first job was scooping ice cream and serving drinks at the mall's only food-selling concession stand. I was later hired and fired from a bridal boutique because I lied and said I knew how to use a computer. Oops. This led to working at Bealls, a department store, throughout high school. It not only brought in money, but I enjoyed the discounts on brand-name clothing. I've since had several jobs: dispatcher for the local sheriff's department and many receptionist positions.

Like most young, carefree teens, I thought I was rolling in money and having a blast. Senior year, I went to South Padre Island for spring break with a family friend and his mom. Our senior trip was to Cancun, Mexico, so I naturally purchased a bikini for each day and saved up plenty of money to splurge—Girbaud, Pepe, Yaga, Guess, and later Rockies and Justin. Life was great. Every now and then, I found myself in a position to help out the family or just pay for lunch or dinner. It felt good to not be a burden once in a while. I thought it was a great start for what was to come.

Wrong. I have made every mistake you can when it comes to money. I obviously had an issue comprehending addition and subtraction. Then came the complications of using checks, thinking credit cards were free money, and considering interest a foreign concept. Bothering Daddy was out of the question, and Mother didn't seem to know much. That left me figuring things out for myself.

When I had Hannah, I was working two jobs to prepare as much as possible for her arrival. With income tax money, I moved out of my parents' house, but that was short-lived. I couldn't afford the mounting bills, diapers, food, etc. Pregnant again, back to my parents' house I went. I did the best I could, attempting to balance all that was happening with no money.

That's when I realized that money does buy happiness. Maybe not love or no-abuse types of happiness, but money would have made being a single mom less stressful. It would have also made things easier for Daddy and me when Mother left. I'm positive money would have helped Mother substantially as well.

When I met Arnie, I was broke (we all know this), but I was indeed working out a plan to get ahead. I had started filling out the registration forms to become a pharmacy technician and was a week into working a cashier job that would eventually lead me to the pharmacy department. I knew every nickel and dime was important, so I applied for WIC to assist me with formula and other items. I lived with Ama by then, and she paid all the bills. It wasn't something I took for granted and tried to quietly pay her back years later.

Arnie made about $2,000 a month as a soldier, which isn't much to support an instant family of four. We managed just fine. Our first dining table may have been a gray-plastic outdoor picnic table from Kmart, but we paid for it ourselves, and we did it together. Throughout the years I scanned yard sales, Craigslist, and later Facebook Marketplace when that became a thing. Cheap or free was how we furnished our duplex and later the first home we purchased in 2006. It was every bit a starter home that needed lots of love. Arnie got to work, and our Trenton home provided years of warmth, growth, and love.

Clothing went from name-brand stuff to clearance and Walmart. It was so easy to find cute, cheap items for the kids, and they always looked adorable. This is how my obsession—shopping on a budget—came to be. It's also the beginning of the story about my husband asking me for a divorce for the first time. Ruh-roh.

This story was totes his fault because he sent me back to Austin while pregnant with Katherine. You know how I told y'all that I had a grand time fucking up Austin with Ama? Well, it didn't come at no cost. The month that Arnie was pissed about was the one in which I spent something like $650 on eating out. I like to say it was an exaggeration, but it really wasn't. (Some of you fancy people may scoff at $650 for the month, when a single meal of yours may have cost more than $650.) I know it was stupid thing for me to do. I had so much fun and don't really regret it. However, I learned not to do it again.

Neither my mother-in-law nor my mother helped with my development of personal perspective on money. My mother-in-law (may she rest in peace) would remind me as often as possible that the money was her son's. It made me very self-conscious about what I spent on myself. See, I was still spending money on the house, kids, and whatever else. I just wasn't spending anything on myself. This caused my self-esteem to take a hit. Due to an unhealed past, it never took much for my self-esteem to plunge.

I stopped wearing makeup, I either cut my own hair or took advantage of the $14.99 special offered at the hair place in the mall, and all my clothes cost ten dollars or less. No, really, I refused to spend more than ten dollars on a dress or pair of jeans and five dollars on a top. Sounds great and all, but most of them were ill-fitting. I bought whatever wouldn't fall off my body. Not great after all. I felt ugly, so I ate. I had plenty of room in my clothes, so I ate more. The more I ate, the fatter I got. I haven't lost the weight, but I have started wearing makeup again and fixing my hair more often. I've also spent years in therapy to heal.

As the kids grew, they got more expensive—such is life. Once we had about one hundred dollars left to our names and about a week left to payday. Arnie and I reverted to our Mexican roots. We bought just enough to make tamales and sold them in the Walmart parking lot. It worked. One thing about us is that, somehow, we are just fine as long as we work together.

Things got better, we outgrew our first home, so we bought our second home. It was when we were buying our third home that Mother came back to bite me in the ass. Arnie received a call from the guy processing our loan to say my credit was shitty. As broke as we were, our bills were paid, and our kids had what they needed. This left us confused. When we went to see what was going on, I found out Mother had rented an apartment, turned on utilities, and bought other things using my name without asking permission, much less telling me. The most fucked-up part was that she stopped paying these things after a couple of months. I was fucking pissed! Of course, she denied it when I confronted her. Regardless, Arnie and I were left with very few options.

Arnie was able to get the loan under his name alone. I was told I could dispute the charges if I filed a police report against my mother. I just couldn't bring myself to file a complaint against her, no matter how awful she had been to me, how many wrongdoings, or how destructive she was. This was a huge hit for many reasons. I'm just thankful she didn't win. We closed on our third home in early 2012. I know our family didn't deserve this situation with my mother, and I know Arnie was beyond pissed, but I've never done anything about it.

Currently, I still enjoy spending money on others and our home. I can't tell you how much I love picking out hostess gifts. Buying a birthday gift for a girlfriend makes me so happy. It's not that I spend hundreds of dollars, because most of them are under twenty dollars, but finding something special that screams their name is what draws me in. I also love buying things for the house. You would think it's decorated to the nines. It's not. Our house is just a home with nothing spectacular about it.

In the last couple of years, Arnie and I have been enjoying more date nights and "going to Lowe's." That's what we tell the kids when we'll be away for the weekend and don't know exactly where we're going.

The clothing? Well, I still have an issue with buying anything full price. I once spent $200 on $1,000 worth of stuff at Belk. Man, I felt like a champ! It's like my Olympics. Strategy, efficiency, and taking no prisoners. I love going item by item in every clearance department. I love finding hidden gems. I especially love to check out the quality of the item and compare it to what it would cost to make it or something similar. It's a whole thing that only Hannah will do with me.

Mother and I had some great times shopping when I lived with her. Ama, mother, Aunt Monica, Hannah, and one of the other little cousins hit yard sales every Saturday morning without fail. I stayed back to get the other three kids fed and ready for the day. Once the ladies made it back, we met up with them and other family members to go shopping. We used to make a full day of it.

One of those special days was on my birthday in 2008. About twenty of us had mobbed up at our nearest discount clothing store when I received a call from Arnie. He was deployed to Afghanistan, and I was expecting him home the following month. Well, he was trying to surprise us by coming home early and buying a truck. He attempted to utilize his mom in the scheme, but it failed. He asked me to go pull out cash from the bank and pay the down payment because the bank wouldn't give his mom the money. Y'all, I started calling out for our troop to reunite in children's clothing to tell them the great news!

There will always be fond memories of shopping with my family. It's not the money being spent, but the time together. There's no time for petty arguments. The kids laugh, play with toys, and always walk out with something new. We ladies talk shit about the blouse someone picked out, watch kids while one of us is nursing, and then all share a meal. The most special parts are the hugs at the end of the day when we all go our separate ways.

So much has changed since then. My favorite aunt passed away, I'm estranged from Mother, and Ama's heart has been broken for many years. No matter how many seconds pass that make those moments further away, I will forever cherish them.

Yes, I'm a red-tag diva with champagne taste on a beer budget. Not sure much would change if I were a millionaire. I truly enjoy the personal time I get with the people with whom I shop. The chatting and getting to know their personal styles. I love the meal. I love the personal quest. For me, shopping goes beyond the store or item purchased.

Chapter Nine

Life Moment: The Day the World Stood Still

Jeez, where do I start? Life hands us moments from the instant we're born. Good, bad, and sometimes neutral until we realize how significant they really were. We don't remember our first embrace or kiss. We don't remember the first time someone told us they loved us. There are times that moments hurt for a second, and others that take a lifetime to recover from…if we are lucky enough to recover.

My earliest memories may have been tainted with fear, but I know there was more to me and my life. I refuse to believe that every smile was fake. The happy times I experienced meant more to me than any negative experience. I've met some incredible people, and I appreciate where I've been. As some women will tell you, the birth of their child(ren) is indescribable in all the best ways. Finding the love of your life isn't a fairy tale, but worth every second. Connecting with someone—or a couple of someones—who becomes more than a friend makes you rich. I have many wonderful people in my life. I am fucking blessed!

However, there is one moment in time… I mentioned it, but didn't fully get into what actually happened. Let me start with the first time I knew mother was incapable of true love. We know how my first pregnancy went, the shit talking, the fucked-up behavior at my baby shower, and the whiplash of hearing good things from mother. When I make it to the finish line and deliver Hannah, the doctor hands her to me, and I am crying uncontrollably. I'm not even going to try and describe that feeling because I'm not smart enough to come up with those kinds of words. Anyway, there I am, holding Hannah and crying.

Mother looks at me and says with a scoff, "Why are you crying? Stop crying. It's just a baby." Those were her words to me, literally.

I remember looking up at Mother and knowing for the first time my feelings about her were right. She didn't love me the way I love my kids because I think she has always been incapable of it. My view is that she was probably a timid person while growing up; from the stories I've heard, Ama was very strict, and her siblings were chaotic at best. She was married prior to Daddy, but that had a tragic ending, and I know she never fully recovered from it. I believe the shock and trauma were never dealt with, and over time she became depressed and extremely anxious. She married Daddy, who, from what I understand, has always been the same person he is today. Probably not what she needed, but she didn't want to be alone, and she wanted to start a family. As we know, that came at a cost. What she thought was going to save her actually destroyed her. Me.

She, like many women, thought, *If someone just loves me, I'll be fine. If I get married, I'll be fine. If I have a baby, it will love me unconditionally…and I'll be fine.*

Those are all lies we tell ourselves when we haven't healed from whatever the fuck has happened. It's complete bullshit to expect another human to give you value. The biggest fucking lie is that babies love their mothers instinctually. Read that again if you need to.

Newborns are instinctually selfish. They have to be in order to survive. They don't care how they get fed. Give them a bottle or a boob. Hell, they don't even care whose boob. They cry to be held. They cry when dirty. They cry when they're sleepy. They fucking cry because they don't like their expensive-ass crib and want to sleep in the thirty-dollar bouncy chair!

So motherhood was the start of just how much my mother had underestimated what she thought she wanted. As stated, mother was a timid, nervous, scared person. She wasn't one to leave the house unless she needed to or had the energy to. You'll know what that's like if you have ever been clinically depressed. Getting pregnant with my baby brother probably complicated things further. It's my understanding that the pregnancy was terrible, and a two-pound, two-ounce baby boy was proof of it. Mother had a premature baby that was sent to a NICU in San Antonio, Texas, two and a half hours away from her. That couldn't have been easy.

Let me add that there have been many rumors that Daddy was engaging in flings. I say flings because an affair, in my mind, is an ongoing situation with the same person. Honestly, I don't know if any of the rumors were ever true. Could they have been? Yes. Has anyone proven them to me? No. Either way, Mother wasn't off to a good start. An active toddler, a newborn preemie, not sure how to describe Daddy, very little money, and a lot of unhealed trauma.

Time passed, and it was becoming clear that I was not what she envisioned as a little girl. I had Daddy's personality and was constantly on the go. She thought I was going to be sweet, calm, and pretty, never messy, and sitting quietly reading a book. Yeah, no. I was everything but. I remember being ornery, feisty, and demanding. Her inability to accept who I was, was taken as a challenge on my part; it only exacerbated the ornery, feisty, and demanding. Lots of big words, actions, and emotions in a little person. I became defiant from an early age and didn't understand why I was such a bad girl for wanting to play. That only progressed as I became a teenager.

This tug of war went on for the rest of our lives. Here's an example of how detrimental things became. When I was about nine or ten years old, and Daddy was working overnight, Mother locked us kids in her bedroom. Not just, "Hey, kids, come sleep in bed with me, and I'll lock the bedroom door." No. The one-thousand-square-foot home had a short hallway dividing the common areas from the bedrooms and bathroom. There was a door at the entrance of the hallway that opened opposite the bathroom door. She tied a belt —or rope, or whatever—to both handles so that one door prohibited the other door's opening. Her bedroom had two windows. One had an air-conditioning window unit, and the other was covered by the headboard of her bed. Because there was space between the foot of the bed and the bedroom door, she slid her dresser in between the two. Then the small space left between the footboard and dresser was filled with drawers from the dresser to minimize the potential of someone breaking in.

This happened every night that Daddy was working. I've never been in jail or prison, but the nights Daddy was home and we got to sleep in our own beds seemed like our one-hour of outdoors time. Not only did I get to see Daddy, but I also got a break from everything that was hurting me. I didn't understand my mother, and things were deteriorating before my eyes.

Mother wasn't good at handling problems or conversations of any sort. There were times she hid at this lady's house when she and Daddy fought. My brother and I didn't know what was going on, other than "Mom is sad." October 1995 was the last time she ran away with my brother and me. After that, she left without us, and we didn't know where she was or when she was coming back.

At some point after I got my driver's license, Daddy and I jokingly reminded each other not to piss off Mom while driving because she would get out of the car at the following traffic light. I think we joked about it because it had happened several times, and we really didn't know how to cope with it. I don't know what Daddy felt, but it hurt me so much.

My mother has always been unpredictable. She was either quiet or explosive. She either liked you or hated you. There's no in between or gray area with her. At least not from my experience. It wasn't until I became a mother that I understood just how broken she was. All her antics came from a deeper place than they appeared. Unfortunately, that didn't get me as far as I wanted it to in reconciling with her.

After she left in December of 2003, things only got worse. This would be the last time she left Daddy. From what I understand, he wasn't having it anymore, and divorce papers were filed. It's difficult to tell my story without divulging details about her personal experience. Although I want to be as open and honest as I can about things, my intention is not to cause her harm. What I can say is that this was the time when roles reversed, and I took on the mother role.

Mother had moved to Austin and had started causing problems. I received a call late one night that required me to drop everything and head to her. Needless to say, she was angry with me. She blamed me for everything. All of it. All the bad. It was a blanket of hate, despair, and persecution, and it weighed thousands of pounds. I was meant to be miserable for all eternity as my penance to her. That didn't go well when I met and later married my husband.

We did the back-and-forth thing for about eight years. She stirred shit up with her siblings and nieces (and I'm not saying they didn't have a hand in the bullshit—that's why I stay the fuck away from them) and decided to get away from them. We took her in, and she stayed with us until she started talking shit to my husband about me, and vice versa. I confronted her, she got pissed, and back to Austin she went. It was a nasty cycle that needed to be broken. Well, the straw that broke the camel's back ended the cycle. Except the pain was only about to begin.

I never imagined what she was capable of. I never thought she would go so far as to destroy her own child. As much as I had seen and experienced with her, I was in no way prepared for her to do what she could to break up my family.

Years have passed since this happened. I still have nightmares about it, and there are times all I can do is nap to keep from crying. In a way, she succeeded in destroying me because I will never be the same again. Maybe some of y'all think this is stupid, but it really did cause tremendous pain. I now live about an hour away from her. I have tried to see her and spend time with her, but I always come home crying. I have spent more time in therapy talking about her than anything else I've gone through.

I feel that grieving her "loss" is challenging in a way that rivals the death of a loved one. Only, she isn't dead. I have to contend with the facts. She *chose* to leave me. She *chose* to cause problems for my husband, me, and our marriage. I can forgive everything else that has happened. I just can't seem to get over this.

Not one thing has ever been the same since this incident. It was as if there had been some type of molecular change in my DNA. Remnants of who I was peek through every once in a while, but it's hard to see how she existed for so long. I feel that I'm harder to love now. I watch everything and everyone with the utmost attention, constantly on high alert. I would rather apologize if I confused an upset belly for gut instinct because I will never not listen to my intuition. I'm scared of fucking up. Like all the time. I'm reminded of my failures and incapacity to be liked, much less loved, every time someone walks out of my life. I often feel petrified as a mom because I don't have anyone to ask and don't know if I'm fucking up. There's just so much.

I wanted a mom. I've needed a mom. I've heard others talk about how wonderful it is to have a mom. My mom was just different. She needed more than she got, I guess. Maybe she just didn't have the strength to pick herself back up. Or maybe she had just been knocked down one too many times.

I have some great memories of Mother; they're just that though. Memories. New ones will never be made. Compartmentalization is how I now try to cope with my pain. I have several boxes I keep for her. One, woman-to-woman. One, she herself is a helpless child. One, mother-to-mother. And the last one, mother-to-child. The first two boxes make things tolerable when I must see her. The other two, I don't know if those will ever heal. Those two people inside me will never understand those two people inside her. Loving someone you hate is an incredibly difficult and daunting burden.

To my mother: I love you. I'm sorry for all that I have done to make things worse. I'm sorry for all you have endured publicly and quietly. I pray your demons let go of their hold so you may find peace, love, and self-acceptance. You were worthy of so much, and I can understand the pain that comes with fighting for that right. Although we may only see each other in passing, I wish you the best.

Chapter Ten

What Do You Want the World to Know about You?

I want the world to know so much, yet nothing at all. It's a ridiculous push and pull of almost needing others to know how hard you're trying, or to be understood, but still not wanting to give one fuck.

I'm a fractured woman gluing herself together one piece at a time. Those fracture lines are a reminder of what I have survived and learned.

I need to remember to speak to myself the way I would speak to someone I love dearly.

I need to love myself the way I love others—unconditionally.

I need to forgive myself the way I forgive those I love.

I need to grow with myself the way I try to grow with my kids.

I need to know that I will not always be as important to someone as they are to me; and that's okay.

I need to know it's okay to have bad days; that doesn't mean it's a bad life or a bad relationship.

I want to learn it's okay to walk away from someone you cared about because they and their actions are toxic—even when it hurts like hell.

I want to remember that my size, wrinkles, and stretch marks don't define me. My laugh lines are a sweet reminder of beautiful moments. My size is just a number on a scale I'll never be happy with, no matter what it tells me. My stretch marks are a lovely reminder that my body brought four extraordinary humans to life.

I want to learn to be mindful of my words.

I want to learn to say no and not be worried about what someone will think of me for it.

I want to learn to not put so much stock into people.

I want to learn how to be patient with myself and others.

I want to learn to control my anxiety and not have it control me.

I want to be strong and truly feel strong.

I want to give to others without depleting myself.

I want to learn that I am worthy. Worthy of happiness. Worthy of true love. Worthy of excitement. Worthy of fulfillment. Worthy of respect. Worthy of peace. Worthy of success. Worthy of life.

I want to remind myself that I don't owe anyone an explanation so long as my husband and children are safe and happy.

I choose to find the good in today.

I choose to find the good in others.

I choose to find the good in lessons.

I choose to find the good in pain.

I choose to find the good in the unknown.

I get lonely.

I get cranky.

I get hyper.

I get needy.

I get aroused.

I get playful.

I get giddy.

I get sad.

I get another day to feel all the feelings and emotions.

I am overprotective.

I am quick to fire back.

I am quick to lose my shit.

I am an overthinker.

Life is obviously unexpected for us all, and there isn't really a right or wrong way to live life so long as you're not causing harm to yourself or others. Tonight, when I was getting closer to finishing this book, our youngest daughter told me she was proud of me. She said, "Don't take this the wrong way, but this will be the first thing you have ever finished. I know how hard it was for you, and I'm extremely proud of you." That was it. That's all I truly ever wanted in life. I wanted to make my family proud, and I may have just done that.

Now, let's see what the other ladies had to say.

Rachael's Beautiful Chaos

Friendship: I am a ride-or-die.

Empowerment: Looking in the mirror and seeing myself.

Dreams: Goals.

Career: Haven't one, but if raising kids paid the maximum, I'd be rich as hell.

Relationship: Shag more than married, but I've been married so long IDK (I don't know).

Offspring: Now I'm stuck with three. I never wanted children to begin with.

Sex: I love playing.

Shopping: Everything—brand whore with a red tag.

Life Moment: When I had to give my youngest CPR after his seizure.

What would you like the world to know about you? That I'm lonely.

Ted's Beautiful Chaos

Friendship: I have two types of friends. I have work buddies whom I enjoy and support at work, but they are not in my life for the long term, so probably not ride-or-die. Then I have my friends whom I consider my family. I may have met them at school, at work, or through other friends. Those people are the ones for whom I would drop everything to help. To me, there is "luv" and "love." "Luv" is temporary and necessary, but "love" is lasting.

Empowerment: Female empowerment is supporting each other and building each other up. It is not supporting women, because we are women. I have to know that I can trust you, and I have to see you doing the best you can. There are women I have refused to support and have fought against because they don't deserve my support. I will stand by and guard your back as long as I can trust you to do the same.

Dreams: Dreams can be a little of all three. I used to dream of being the tambourine girl in a rock band—my fantasy. Dreams with a plan are goals that can become reality with hard work and belief in myself. I have found that when I commit to a dream and make a plan to follow up, it becomes my reality.

Career: My career was my first dream that became my reality. I love my career! Teaching is my passion! Children make me happy, drive me crazy, and make me strive to be a better me. After thirty-one years, I still love it, I still get excited in August, and I am spending this summer working and studying so that I will be better next year. To me, everyone has to work, so you should do the work that you love.

Relationship: I have been married to the same crazy man for thirty-two years. We have been together for thirty-five. Not sure what a shag is, but I think he was it before I married him. He is also the one I have wanted to kill at different points on this coaster ride. He is my friend, my lover, and my other half. My celebrity shag would be George Strait, even as he is now, and Harrison Ford when he was younger. Celebrity I would kill—well, just say I don't care to see anyone related to, married to, given birth by any of the Kardashians.

Offspring: I have two beautiful children. I look back at how I raised them and wish I had made other choices, but they are two of the most amazing adults, so I guess we didn't do too bad. Best thing I have ever done in my life was to have Chelsea and Jarred. They are truly my gifts from God.

Sex: Sex! What a question to ask your teacher! Sex is a great part of my marriage. Enjoy it as much as I did when we were a whole lot younger.

Shopping: Brand-name whore with perfume! I love a great perfume. I will mortgage my house for a great perfume. Otherwise, I shop the cheap aisle.

Life Moment: The two days I first met my babies definitely count as take-my-breath-away days. Their beautiful faces, their tiny fingers, and the love that overtook my body and soul are experiences I will never forget. The two worst days of my life are when my brother and mother-in-law passed away. Getting the phone call about Brad, I collapsed on the floor and can still hear myself screaming. When the doctors told me about my mama Stella, and I realized that

I was now the one responsible for telling my husband and father-in-law that she was gone…I did what I always do. I called my mama, and she talked me through it. Those four days—the best and the worst ones of my life.

What would you like the world to know about you? I would want the world to know that I probably care too much. That I wish everyone would care too much. I put others first way too much, and I struggle with many things. I fight with wanting to do things for me and wanting to please others. Usually, I end up not getting what I want. This is my life's battle.

Juanita's Beautiful Chaos

Friendship: Ride-or-die.

Empowerment: Power, courage, and success.

Dreams: Reality and goals.

Career: Jesus is always there.

Relationship: No answer given to Shag. Boris Kodjoe, I'd marry him. And kill Kanye.

Offspring: Hell no.

Sex: Grapefruit.

Shopping: Red-tag brand whore.

Life Moment: When I was able to provide for my daughter at sixteen.

What would you like the world to know about you? I'm obnoxiously weird. HA HA!

Emily's Beautiful Chaos

Friendship: I am very careful with the word "friendship." I have two cousins who have been my friends since the first grade. I'm a ride-or-die to those two, but the rest are just acquaintances, people I just hang out with, but with whom I have no real connection. I was raised by my grandfather; he taught me that my cousins were my friends, and that wholeheartedly stayed with me.

Empowerment: Female empowerment is that, when we move up in life, we should look back and help other women up as well. I mentor younger women on how to take a step above. It's not about getting there and not showing a younger woman how to do the same. It's about lifting up other females. I was a volunteer speaking to pregnant teens about life choices. In a group of girls just listening to what I had to say to get free stuff, I cherished the one who stuck around after to get more information. That one girl can make a change for not only herself, but for her child. It can be liberating to know that my story can make a change for good.

Dreams: Reality can manifest in a dream. Mine happened to come to me seven years after my nightmare. It was time for me to face reality and move forward. We were raped by an uncle and had the same experiences. It wasn't until the dreams or nightmares started that we all discovered that we each went through it. The three of us helped to heal each other from a horrible past.

Career: I went to school, and I got the job I thought I wanted. I'm a nurse, and I moved up pretty quickly. I made a lot of money and worked a lot of overtime. I'm now forty-seven and married. Now my job is just my job. I'm a wife first, a mother second, and then a nurse. I was the person who worked every shift they gave me. It was all about being a nurse. Today it's just a job.

Relationship: I'm a newlywed of a year and a half. This is my third marriage, and he has taught me how to be a wife. My first marriage was when I was seventeen, and I had two kids. He was verbally, physically, and mentally abusive. This was while I was in nursing school. The second marriage, I don't know why I got married to him. I think he was gay. We were married ten years, but he was only around for two years. He used to volunteer for overseas assignments.

I met my third husband in 2015, and he changed my life. The first two marriages taught me how to appreciate what he is as a husband. HE taught me how to communicate with him. He knows me so well that my hello tells him how my day went. I was able to own my feelings. Then I was able to learn to love myself. He was there every step of the way.

Shag: Beyonce

Marry: Denzel Washington

Kill: Kim and Kanye West

Offspring: I have two kids, but I didn't want them at the time I had them. I was a teenager, but didn't believe in abortions, so I had them. When I had her, she changed my whole life. We had nothing for her, and I used to tell her that all she had was love. That's all we had. My first child and I slept on a sofa in my aunt's house for the first year of her life. We had nothing.

My grandfather would tell me that I made things harder for myself, but that it was doable. I wasn't the first teen to get pregnant, and I wouldn't be the last.

Now they are both nurses, and I'm so proud of them. They came from humble beginnings, and they both have college degrees.

Sex: Right now, I'm forty-seven and having the best sex of my life. It's the husband that I have and our communication. He tells me what he wants, and I tell him what I want. We also have our "not happening" list. We try to make it happen at least every other day. Before him, sex was just something you do. I feel as if now that I know my body, I'm experiencing sex for the first time.

Shopping: What I do is shop for what I want. I don't shop a lot. I can treat myself well. Call that whatever you want.

Life Moment: The most drastic thing that happened to me was Hurricane Katrina. I went to work, and the next thing you know I was getting airlifted. I couldn't find my kids, we lost our home, and I felt the politicians let us all sit in a city drowning in water. There should have been no reason to leave us for five days. I saw some crazy shit that never made the news. Then I didn't know what would happen next after being brought to a city in which I knew no one. We didn't know where we were going. It was all just sit and wait, with all the uncertainty of the world. Being called a refugee in my own state made me angry. I think there needs to be more done for natural-disaster victims.

What would you like the world to know about you?
People can change. People deserve second chances. And it's not where you come from, but where you're going. I know I'm a totally different person than I used to be.

Dolores's Beautiful Chaos

Friendship: I am an awesome fucking friend. My friends will tell you the same. I'm honest and will tell you exactly what you need to hear. I refuse to spoil you because you feel it's required. I will drop everything to fly out to you and make your day better. We will bullshit and lift you up, but I'm not bullshitting you. On the other hand, I won't take your bullshit. I will drop you for it. This works both ways for me.

Empowerment: Being able to do you without feeling guilt or shame. There shouldn't be a double standard. It's not just about intelligence, sexuality, or careers. It's about having all that you want without remorse, regret, shame, or feeling conflicted. Most importantly, without giving up your sense of identity.

Dreams: Once I set my mind to something, consider it done. If l bring my idea to you, it's just to shoot the shit.

Career: As a kid, I wanted to be everything. As you get older and learn about yourself, those dreams become "fuck that shit." At one point, I wanted to be a nurse, as I came from a long line of nurses. It's when my grandfather had skin cancer that I became his nurse. I knew then that would be my only patient. After trial and error, and at the tender age of forty-one, I still don't know what I want to be when I grow up.

Relationship: I'm married, but I feel as if I shouldn't be. I'm very independent. He is way too sensitive, and I blame our upbringing. I love the idea of marriage. I love having someone to come home to at night. But I like to be alone physically and with my thoughts. It's unconventional, and that works for me. Don't get me wrong, I love my husband. I've just lived with myself longer.

Shag: Michael B. Jordan

Marry: Don Cheadle

Kill: Brad Pitt or Kevin Hart

Offspring: After three kids, I feel underappreciated. Do I want more? Fuuuuuuuuuuuck nooooooo! I like watching them grow into who they are, but it's also sad. I mean that outside influences sometimes overshadow what we have instilled in them. Sometimes it's hard to sit back and let them fight their own battles, but as parents we have to be still and let them fight their own battles.

Sex: It's obligatory for me. It used to be down and dirty, couldn't get enough, several times a day. However, due to a disability, I just can't bring myself to feel it.

Shopping: I'm somewhere in between. I like brand names but want a good deal. I don't remember the last thing I bought myself. All my money goes to my six foot four, fifteen-year-old, size-15 shoe-wearing son. He needs a job.

Life Moment: When I let go of everything. After my divorce, I started meditating, and I let go of all the hatred and anxiety, and started mending fences. That's when I reconnected with myself and healed. Out of the ugly came life.

What would you like the world to know about you? I'm strong on the outside and carry a lot on my shoulders. The inside is very fragile. Sharing your vulnerability can be very empowering.

Mary's Beautiful Chaos

Friendship: I like to think that once we're friends, we're friends. I feel as if it's harder to make friends once you're married and have kids. My husband and I are blunt, and maybe that's why it's hard. We'll hang out with couple friends, and then they don't want to hang out anymore. I have a friend from high school who moved away to become a physician's assistant. She was my best friend. Her husband passed away a year ago (at the time of the interview), and things just haven't been the same. We hang out with family members the most and have dinners. You can be friends with the opposite sex with the trust of your spouse.

Empowerment: I think women shouldn't be putting women down in any way. We are put down in jobs and for the way we dance on TikTok. That teaches our kids that it's okay to put others down in school. I think it's good to boost anyone up—women, kids, whatever—whether it's in school, online, or in the workplace. We go through enough stuff as it is with the way we look or our jobs.

Dreams: I don't remember any dreams when I was a kid, but I have dreams now. I wish I had all the money in the world and a huge house. That's a big dream, but I guess it's possible. Will it take me forever? Yeah, probably. It would make me happy because I feel I wouldn't have to worry so much or live paycheck to paycheck. Am I going to have enough for bills or this or that? I really want this purse, but can I afford it? My parents can want something and just go buy it. I want that. That's how I was raised, and I want to live it again one day.

Career: I always wanted to be a doctor, a surgeon. That's why I've been watching *Grey's Anatomy*. I watch shows about surgeries and autopsies on TV and Instagram. I just think that stuff is so cool. I didn't do it because I'm horrible at school. I barely passed. I was going to school for teaching, but because I was so horrible at college, I dropped out. My mom is a hairstylist, and I use to go to hair shows with her. So I went to school for it and now work for my mom. I do like that I get paid to sit and gossip with people. It ended up working out for the best, and I love it. I make my own schedule, and it works with the kids. I also get to be creative. I don't get to cut people open, but I get to cut something.

Relationship: I'm all for marriage, and we met on a dating site. Come to find out, our families go to church, bowl, and dine together. He had a daughter, and now we have been together almost ten years, married for almost six. I love him to death, but I want to kill him sometimes. I tell him the only way he's getting out is in a box.

Marry: Chris Hemsworth

Shag: Ryan Reynolds

Kill: Tom Cruise

Offspring: Mary, my daughter, is ten, and my son is three; I had three miscarriages in between. There is no way in hell I'm having anymore. If he gets me pregnant again, I'll chop his wiener off. I have my boy, I have my girl, and I'm done; they are way too expensive. My miscarriages were all pretty early. One had a sac and no baby when we went in for our ultrasound. The second ones were twins. We went in for an ultrasound right before Christmas, and they saw that something was wrong with one, but the other could possibly survive. I started bleeding and clotting. I lost it. The doctors wanted to wait to see if they would make it. I was given pills in case I started losing the other one because I didn't want a D&C. I woke up Christmas Eve in a lot of pain and couldn't get out of bed, so my husband carried me to the bathroom. That's when I lost the second twin.

Christmas Eve is usually hard for me. I still went to church that night, and cry every year when the memories come back. I didn't have support then, or now, for losing my babies. My mother told me it was just the way it was meant to be. My husband just doesn't acknowledge I was ever pregnant. My sister-in-law has fertility issues, but we don't talk about it together. The only person who talks about them is my daughter when she mentions that her brother(s) or sister(s) are in heaven.

Sex: Hell yeah! The more, the better. My husband…some days I want him more than others, and he gets mad at me. So he likes it every day. I can't do that much; my vagina would hurt. He would like to try all this new stuff, and I'm open to trying some of it. He wants to try a new hole, but I think things should only come out of your butthole. I like role playing, trying things, and wearing sexy things. I have a little drawer. I like to surprise him, but it's hard when you have two kids running around.

So, last night, my husband was lying on the floor (fully clothed), and I sat on him, as I have done before. Our daughter says to me, "Mommy, you're sitting on Daddy's privates! You can't do that. Get off!"

Shopping: I'm both. I really love me some Michael Kors. I'm really picky about my purses, but not my clothes. I shop at Walmart for my clothes. It's just my purses that I'm crazy about.

I don't know; I've never thought about being a brand whore. I love yoga pants, leggings, and tank tops. That's what I wear, but no specific brand.

Life moment: I think dealing with my daughter and everything that comes with dealing with her mother. Everything I've had to deal with in the past with her mom has made me grow as a person, has tested me, and has made my husband's and my relationship stronger. Basically, she is the baby momma from hell. We used to be friends, and then it went to hell. Now she doesn't see her daughter, and I've raised her since she was a year and a half. It really changed me.

What would you like the world to know about you? Basically, everything I have done I've done for my kids. I hope they have a good life and that they know I love them.

Malory's Beautiful Chaos

Friendship: I am a die-hard loyalist, but don't have that many close friends. I recently had to cut ties with my best friend; we'd been friends since I was five. I have many acquaintances and can talk to anyone. The people who are closest to me know me the best; I'm an open book, but keep a few chapters to myself.

Empowerment: I'm definitely a bystander. I think female empowerment is being proud of being the woman you are and not feeling defined by limitations.

Dreams: I think dreams guide you in a direction in your life. I have some goals that I want to get to, and I'm slowly getting there. I want to learn and quit my job to learn woodworking. I want to create things that others will appreciate. But I wouldn't do it because my family would ridicule me. I'm a bigger girl, not just in weight, but I have broad shoulders and what I call man hands. If I started woodworking, they would just make it really hard for me. I'm taking a class in woodworking as a treat to myself for my birthday. I also crochet, knit, and quilt. I love making things and giving them away, especially to my students.

*Author's Note: You can feel the love and emotion in this woman's desire to give to others. It's quite profound and beautiful.

Career: This is what I've always wanted to do. I have always wanted to be a teacher. After high school, I didn't have the means to go to college, so I joined the Air Force. I taught pilots how to use their safety equipment. I got out, worked different jobs, and then got pregnant. I was fired from one job because they said my being a single mother "did not mesh well with their company." So then l actually applied for TANF (Temporary Assistance for Needy Families) and was denied because they said I made too much money; I made $600 a month. That's when I moved in with my mother and got my four-year degree in three. I have now been teaching for ten years.

Relationship: I guess I would be in the kill stage. I chose that because I just got divorced. Happily divorced. My ex-husband had to control everything. Our final fight was about a broken couch and my wanting to go buy a new one. That turned into him telling me I only want to spend money, asking if I was cheating on him, and on and on. It was the last time. I told him to pack his shit and get out. Eventually I'll date again, but I don't think I need a man in my life to be happy.

Offspring: So there's a story. I always wanted children. I had female problems and was told I was never going to have kids. I went to the doctor because I didn't feel well, just to find out I was pregnant. It was a difficult pregnancy, and I was on bed rest for six months. I also found out he was cheating on me and left him when I was five months pregnant. I love her so much, but I need her to go to a friend's house for the weekend and let me stay home by myself.

Sex: I can say I was molested for two years by my neighbor, and then I was raped by my sister's friend. I thought I wanted it as I grew, but now I can do with or without it. I had lost my attraction to my husband, so it became "let's just do it so I can get back to my show." I want my point of view to change. I think, when I find the right one and thoroughly bond with someone, it will be what I want.

Shopping: I'm totally a red-tag diva! I'm totally cheap and know how to shop. Amazon is like crack for me. I like the thrill of the hunt, but I grew up poor. So I always wonder, *What if something happens?* The older I get, I realize if I buy something from Walmart, it's cheap and won't last as long. Now I spend a little more, but wait for those sale emails.

Life Moment: I can think of two moments. The first one was when I attempted suicide. When I had all my female issues, it went to shit, and there wasn't the help that I needed. Now it makes me appreciate life and to know that things are really never that bad.

Also sad, in March, we had a student go missing. We rallied teachers to search for this child. We were supposed to go out Thursday, but ended up waiting until Friday. I found her. I found her with the gun still under her leg. She'd died the day before. All I wanted to do was go to church and pray. I needed that. COVID had just hit, and the churches were closed. I stood there, waiting for an hour until I found a priest to pray with me.

Some of my peers and I got really drunk that night, and when I got home, I saw my daughter waiting for me outside. We just looked at each other for a moment, and then we hugged. It's a hug I will never forget.

When I got back to my classroom, I took the student's chair out because I couldn't look at it anymore. I have since started therapy, and I'm being treated for PTSD.

What would you like the world to know about you? Okay, so I put on a strong face, and it's legit. But sometimes it hurts. It hurts the way they look at you, but I don't want the world to see it hurts. You know that saying about God only giving you what you can handle? Well, I can handle it and would rather do it, so someone else doesn't have to.

*Author's Note: We need more Malorys in this world. Today I cried with a stranger, and it was comforting.

Stephanie's Beautiful Chaos

Friendship: Somewhere in the middle. If you are good to me, I am good to you. If you betray me, then I'll stay an acquaintance, but I won't pick you up at the airport. You'll remain a Facebook friend. My ride-or-die can call me anytime, anywhere, and I'll be there. I'll be on my way to you.

Empowerment: I think of it in terms of the men at the mechanic shop and how they speak to us as if we're stupid. Or the landscape guy who can't take orders from the little housewife who, in reality, knows exactly what they are talking about. I don't need a pink vagina on my head, but I do think respect goes a long way for both sexes. It's not about belittling what I don't know, but educating me to know more. Just because we are women, that doesn't mean we don't know what you know.

Dreams: I never had dreams of being a doctor or anything like that. I had smaller accomplishments that I wanted to achieve because I was told I couldn't. So when everyone told me I couldn't be a model, and my ex told me I was too ugly, I went and did it. I left him and the baggage behind. I became a model, I have a high IQ, I have powerlifted, and I've checked off all the things I wanted.

My husband once asked me what I wanted to be. My answer was available. He asked me what that meant. I told him I wanted to be available for those who need me—our church, the garden group, or my family. Now he calls me a professional volunteer.

Career: I tried school; I tested out my junior year of high school. Thereafter, I've lived life doing whatever someone said I couldn't do.

Relationship: My husband and I have shared eighteen years together and have been married for seventeen. He's awesome. We don't fight. We disagree, we argue, but we don't fight. Most importantly, he lets me be me.

Shag and Marry: Sam Elliott

Kill: Hillary Clinton, but I just want to pour hot coffee on her. I can't kill anyone.

Offspring: All our kids are out of the house, and we only have four-legged furbabies—by the way, cats. My husband wants a dog, but I'm not sure my babies would be okay with that.

Sex: It's eighteen-year sex. I love knowing this is the one person I get to be with for the rest of my life.

Shopping: Let's go! It depends on the item. Sometimes you get what you pay for. I'm quality over quantity. I love shopping at thrift stores and antique shops. Accidental Beadist on Etsy [her favorite shop].

Life Moment: Bad was the day my first husband banged my head into the wall after I had been to the dentist. He was mad because he told me I couldn't go, but I went in for a toothache. That was the day I was out.

The best day of my life was my first kiss from my dear Harry. I can still feel the butterflies just talking about it.

What would you like the world to know about you? I'm not sure how to answer this, but I just want my kids to know I did my best.

Ruth's Beautiful Chaos

Friendship: Friendship means a lot to me. Friendship is a very sacred thing. I don't make friends easily, so when I do, I don't think I'm territorial, but may be possessive. When I get there, I don't want anyone butting into that area. I'm very much that person who, when you're my friend, is going to throw herself in front of you and protect you. Right or wrong, no one is going to change that. It also gets me hurt quite a bit. I put more in than I receive, so I have more of an expectation than what others are willing to give.

As I have gotten older, I've become more antisocial, private, and selective with whom I allow in my world. I wouldn't say this has helped me in a healthy way, but I don't get hurt as easily. Now I'm always looking for the red flags. I only have one friend whom I've had since childhood. Then there was another who passed away a few years ago. I am now a caregiver for a gentleman who has Alzheimer's and another form of dementia. He is my ride-or-die because he gives me advice and then forgets what I told him.

*Author's Note: Prior to starting our interview, Ruth spoke so highly, genuinely, and with such affection for this man she has cared for, for the past five years. From what I gather, it has become a real alliance between two unsuspecting humans living life as best they can.

Empowerment: Let me tell you about the empowerment of women: I don't give a shit about women's empowerment!

I didn't ask for it. I was perfectly happy staying home and taking care of my kids. I didn't have to worry about equal pay, equal treatment. I don't think women can ever be equal to men. There's a reason why a man is a man, and a woman is a woman. I have no problem being feminine and playing the feminine role. I'm okay with women being equal to men if that is what they want. They can be the same in employment or at home. I'm just not the one to chase the women's empowerment movement.

When I was about fourteen years old and talking to my grandmother, she asked me, if there was one thing in history I could change, what would it be. I looked at her and said, "In all honesty, I would go back in time and assassinate Susan B. Anthony because I didn't ask for any of this. I didn't ask to vote. I didn't ask for anything. I would have been home, happy with my kids."

She looked at me with utter disappointment, and she probably wondered where she went wrong with me. She was adopted and lived a very comfortable and privileged life. She also went to college. My answer was probably the last thing she thought I would say. This conversation comes from a woman who drank boxed wine and a child who was politically incorrect. She was my rock.

Ten years later, and it's [her grandmother's passing] still devastating to me.

Dreams: I grew up being a very cynical and smart-ass child. As my grandmother would say, I have no tact. If I think it, I will say it before my face would have revealed it. I didn't believe in miracles or fairy tales. I didn't believe in marriage. I remember having a conversation with my dad in which he asked me when I planned on getting married. My response to him was, "Why? It cost fifty dollars to get married, then thousands to get divorced. I can just live in sin and be just as happy." He wasn't happy with that response. Outside of this, I don't know that I have a view on what dreams mean.

Growing up as I did, there was nothing positive to look forward to. I didn't have a parental role model who told me I needed to make plans to be more or have dreams. I was told to go outside to play while they lived their lives. I didn't have the structure with which to build a life. I didn't have dreams or goals of a career, and then I got pregnant.

My dreams and goals came when I lost both my parents to cancer. That's when I knew what direction I wanted to take. They both died of the same cancer. One was due to being a smoker, but the other was not. My mom was forty-nine, and my dad was sixty.

Career: I wouldn't say I had a career because I thought it was just a job. Looking back, I didn't for twenty years, so now I would say it was. But my career is now. Working in the medical field. I will continue to work towards it, and I want to work with cancer patients.

Relationship: I don't have a relationship. I don't even have a FWB. [Author's Note: I didn't know what FWB was—friends with benefits.] Right now, I'm just focused on my career and taking care of my kids. I'm open to it, but men lie. They say they aren't married, but… Or the men who still live with their moms… I just can't.

The thing about this that sucked is that my ex was able to move on after two months. We lived together for ten years and had three kids. I would describe this relationship as volatile and toxic. After infidelity, alcoholism, drug use, physical abuse, and the rest, I just couldn't do it anymore. His dreams and goals were not mine. It was when the numb feeling set in that I knew this was the end.

Shag: Sam Elliott

Marry: I don't want to marry anyone. At this point in my life, I'm much more comfortable being alone.

Kill: I have a list.

Offspring: I have seven children: six boys and one girl. I was pissed when I found out I was pregnant with the last. He wanted another child, and I didn't. He eventually convinced me. I don't want to say I didn't want *her*, but I didn't want to be pregnant. Now I have ten grandchildren and am happy for the way it worked out. I get pissy when they don't all come over and hang out with me. I miss my kids being little and having Mommy moments. I miss the cuddles and love.

Sex: I would say being molested had an impact when I was younger. It was a hard thing because my dad was my molester. I was always on pins and needles growing up. I was my sisters' protector and would get in the middle so he wouldn't hurt them. When I got older, I didn't really know what sex was about. It was just something I did. Even when I was married for ten years, it was emotionless sex. There was nothing. I didn't know what it was to be made love to. Now there is some emotion, and I can enjoy it, but I still look for the red flags. I have a wall up because I don't want to get hurt.

Shopping: Am I a shopper? No. I do love my pants from Target, but I don't buy a lot. I found SHEIN, and I buy my daughters' and my clothes from there. I really am a shoe junkie! My daughter makes fun of me and says I have

200 pairs of Filas. Then I tell her, "Now I have 201." I think the shoes stem from my childhood. My dad was cheap and would only buy cheap shoes and tell us that we had to make them last. We would get them at thrift stores or dollar stores. I always envied the kids who had K-Swiss. I always wanted those. It wasn't that he didn't have money, he was just cheap as hell.

Life Moment: I just think, for me, growing up in an abusive home and being molested started the structure of the dynamics for how my life would go. Who really put me on the path to where I was going was my grandma. That's why I always stayed where I was. What if she needed me? I could have gone at any time to see her. If my grandma wouldn't have been around, I probably wouldn't have my kids. I would have left. But she was my world, and I couldn't leave her. That is why my younger sister won't talk to me. She gets upset because I refer to her as "my" grandma. My sister says she was all of ours. But, no, she was mine. When my grandma was in hospice, she was in a coma. My cousin and I were arguing over whom she belonged to. She woke up and told us to both shut up. We jokingly blamed each other, but she was still my grandma because I was her favorite.

What would you like the world to know about you? That I'm human. I have feelings. I have compassion. I have hope. I'm just like you. When you see yourself in the mirror, you see me too.

Earth Angel's Beautiful Chaos

Friendship: I think I'm a very good friend. If I say I'm going to be there, I'll be there. I know things come up, but it drives me nuts for people to not show up and be flaky. That personality trait doesn't sit well with me. I know things come up, but every time? Due to moving often, I don't have friendships that ended badly, but they just drifted apart. I had a friend in Maryland, and we used to show up at each other's houses with no notice. Nothing was ever planned; things naturally flowed. We were both stay-at-home moms, and she is the only one I had that was a true friendship, and before C-19 we used to see each other at least once a year. Everyone else has been an acquaintance.

I feel as if my husband is my best friend and person, but it's nice to have someone to do things with when he is busy or isn't interested. Recent struggles with my daughter's mental health have taken a toll on both of us, but I have had to carry a heavier load because he is triggered by her anxiety and depression because of his PTSD. It would be nice to have someone I can confide in when I'm trying to shield him from all the negative feelings. Instead, I have had to utilize counseling as an outlet for my emotions. I don't talk to others about what we are going through and open a can of worms because I don't want them to change their perception of us or our daughter.

Empowerment: I don't consider myself a feminist; I believe that women are capable of doing anything they want to do. I think women's empowerment is just teaching girls that they can do whatever they want to do and not be just what is between their legs. I believe some of the things; I like traditional gender roles, but I don't like to be limited by them. For the most part, I take care of the inside of the house, and my husband does yard work. That's not to say he can't come inside and clean while I go outside and mow the lawn. We don't have to stick with roles.

Dreams: I feel I have surpassed any dream I had when I was younger. What I have accomplished, the family I have. So now my dreams are geared toward continuing to be comfortable and happy. To me, comfort and happiness means not worrying about money or health. I would like to travel more, experience other cultures, and see new things.

Career: I've known I wanted to be in the medical field since I was a kid. In seventh grade, I discovered occupational therapy, and it's been what I wanted to do since then. I finally got my master's degree at age thirty and have been an occupational therapist for the past fifteen years...and still love it!

Relationship:

Shag: Morris Chestnut

Marry: Morris Chestnut

Kill: Donald Trump

I've been married for twenty-three years, and we have a wonderful relationship with great communication. We have had struggles and have seen the bottom, wondering if it was the end of our marriage at times. At the beginning of our marriage, he would go out a lot and release his stress from work and family, but we had had our son. I had already transitioned into being a wife and mother and wasn't interested in the party life. If he was a husband and dad, why did he need to go out? He wondered what was wrong with that. That created a division. I didn't protest it as much as I should have. I didn't know how to verbalize how or why it was hurting me.

Trying for our second child, we were having infertility issues, and I had two miscarriages. This caused even more issues in our marriage. I didn't blame him for our infertility issues, but he took on the burden of not being able to give me what I wanted. I didn't know about his struggles at the time. I found out years later that it was a chore for him to have sex with me. He revealed that my wanting a baby took the fun and intimacy away from our sex life.

Not knowing how he was feeling created a further wedge and led to infidelity on his part. That infidelity led us to counseling, and that is when he told me. I knew the grass wasn't greener on the other side; no marriage is without struggles. I knew I didn't want to struggle with anyone else, and that is what helped me stay in my marriage and work through things.

What has helped us is not just learning to communicate, but knowing how each of us communicates. I have learned that he doesn't tell me everything, but it's not because he is hiding it. It's because he either doesn't see it as important, or he doesn't want me to stress out about his work. I think we have great communication, but I think we have to be conscientious about the rules of our communication. For example, if he tells me something went wrong at work, I have to keep my anger towards his coworker to myself. Sometimes good communication means being a passive listener. I believe that our communication has been the biggest tool for making our marriage work. If you can talk about it, you can work on it.

Offspring: We are done having children! We got married in May, and I was pregnant by June, so we haven't had a time in our marriage where it was just about us. We're excited to be empty nesters and not have to consider them in our plans. We will always worry about them, but it will be great to enjoy us.

Sex: At the beginning of our relationship, we were very sexually active. He has had a very high sex drive throughout our marriage until recently. I, on the other hand, had a lower libido. He was the one who usually initiated, and that's where the problem came in. Having sex three times a week is a lot for someone with a lower sex drive, and it never gave me the chance to be the initiator, as my husband would have liked for me to be every once in a while. I also feel that I needed more foreplay, as I would just be getting started when he was ready to finish.

However, currently the roles have changed. He has been taking medication that has made his sex drive take a nosedive. At first, I thought there must be something bothering him, something I wasn't doing, or there was someone else. I remember feeling as if he was punishing me, or as if it was a game for him to prove a point. As if he was trying to see how long I'd go without, or how long it would take me to initiate. When I finally approached him about it, he assured me that it was just the medication and that he still found me sexy.

His love language is physical touch, which made the change so shocking. Now we still hug and cuddle, we have sex once a week, and things are great as far as I'm concerned. It started off embarrassing to ask for what we wanted, and now we are both very open to trying new things or toys.

Shopping: I am not a shopper. I have a few brand-name items, but I have a hard time spending the money on things. Why should I spend more money for a label if the purse looks the same? We have always been pretty thrifty and cautious about money, which allows us to make the big purchases easily. We don't have to worry about money, but that's because our day-to-day spending is mindfully controlled.

Life Moment: I wish I could say this was a happy event. That one thing was facing and contemplating divorce. What did that look like? What were the changes we would face? That made me fight harder for my marriage. It wasn't what I wanted. I wanted him. It wasn't a happy moment, but ultimately it made for a happy life.

What would you like the world to know about you? I'm kind. I care about others and that they are happy. Yet I am easily annoyed by others—the unkind, self-serving, or flaky. I feel I am very empathetic and want everyone to get along, but I am very judgmental if people don't have those same qualities.

Veronica's Beautiful Chaos

Friendship: I'm definitely a long-term friend. I don't like the ones in and out. That's draining to me. My friendships are very important to me. For the most part, I like to just go with the flow, and I don't expect much, but I like to know where I stand with people. I think I make myself pretty clear about where I stand as well. Communication is very important to me. I don't like to not know.

Empowerment: Female empowerment is supporting each other any way we can without judgment. Of course, with the exception of being a shitty person. I hate that people make it out to be on their terms. As if you are only supporting them when you believe in what they are doing. We have come so far from misogyny; we shouldn't be the ones setting ourselves back.

Dreams: I think they are goals. I don't think dreams are too outrageous, unless they're about unicorns. I think you can always get that dream job if you work hard. I think all dreams can become reality; some just take more time and effort than others. I also don't think we should discourage people for their dreams. I think it's a mental thing. They are getting in their own way. People are going to talk shit about you anyways, so you might as well do it.

Career: The paths I wanted to take in my life have changed so many times. When I was in middle school, I thought I was going to be a lawyer, or a detective and solve murder mysteries. Now, if I had the perfect career, I would marry a trillionaire, with my four kids, and be a model and sell overpriced breast pumps to my Instagram followers, who would get ten percent off their purchase using my code.

Unfortunately, my future husband hasn't come to save me from this hell, so I'm currently looking for a more stable job. I don't know how I feel about a career, other than wanting something that will take care of me comfortably, even if that means doing something I don't like. I don't know what I want to do, and that's why I'm just getting by for now.

Relationship: Where am I in my life? I just don't want to deal with anyone's bullshit, if I'm being quite frank. I talk to so many guys, and I don't know any of their favorite colors, nor do I care. A lot of times, guys just want to have sex, and I'm not here for that. I don't expect my significant other to be perfect. I would actually appreciate the opposite. I just want someone who will be willing to put in the effort. I think everything else will fall into place if I'm truly whom they want. I feel as if I would be more accepting of other people's faults than the other way around. I think it would be easier for me to see the ugly in them and stay, than for them to see the ugly in me and stay. I think a relationship can be a beautiful thing. I think they can be healthy. I also think having a healthy relationship is harder than having a toxic one.

*Author's Note: When asked why, she stated that in a toxic relationship, you sweep everything under the rug. You have to work towards a healthy relationship. She also said she is sleep-deprived and will probably disagree with herself in the morning.

Shag: Chris Evans

Marry: Charlie Hunnam

Kill: Adam Levine and the mistress

Offspring: I actually love and hate kids, all at the same time. My ideal number of kids is probably four. If I had a fifth one, I would have to have a sixth one because odd numbers aren't going to work for me. I think I would rather have kids when I'm younger than older because I don't want to be the mom mistaken for the grandmother. But I also don't want to be too young, where I'm learning to wipe my ass and their ass at the same time. You know what I mean? I think it's extremely important to me to be as emotionally stable as I can be. I want to be as emotionally available as possible for them. I don't want them to go a day wondering if they are loved or needed. I don't want them to need attention from somewhere else because they aren't getting it at home.

If I think if I've learned anything by working at a day care, it is how mean adults can be to little kids. That's insane to me. As a caregiver, how can you be so mean and judgmental to little kids who don't know anything or know better. They aren't even trying to be annoying. I never want to put my kids in day care.

I also think adults allow their emotions to dictate how they treat the kids. I also think there are a lot of bad parents. Not misunderstood parents—just really bad parents.

Sex: I've never done it, so…I have no advice, and sometimes I still think it's gross, like in middle school. I'll probably, if anything, wait for marriage. I just had my first kiss, and I'm twenty years old. I don't know. I think sex is kind of funny.

Shopping: I love shopping. It's very therapeutic. I would go shopping every day if I could. I could spend a grand or two in a day with no problems. If I had enough money in the moment, I would just buy it and not try it on. It would just happen. I just really love to spend money. I get annoyed when I don't have money. I don't like seeing the money leave my bank account, but I like what I buy. If I don't touch my money, it will stay that way. The second I spend even one dollar, it's all over.

Life Moment: No answer given.

What would you like the world to know about you? I overthink a lot. 'Cause there are a lot of times I could have avoided problems if I hadn't been overthinking. Also, if I ever hurt anyone's feelings in a cruel way, I'm sorry. I didn't mean to. I want people to know I'm trying my best, even if I don't know what I'm doing.

Theresa's Beautiful Chaos

Friendship: For me, it's hard because I'm an Army brat. I have two ride-or-die friends from high school, but there are very few I take along, going from one duty station to another. I have friends with whom I have a connection for just that duty station, and when three years are up, the friendship is up. Now we've settled in one spot since my husband retired, but I don't know if I'm ready for another commitment. I have friends here and there, but my girls are back home, and things just fit every time I go back to how we left them.

Empowerment: I'm definitely big on this because of my background. My dad lived on a small farm and was raised by a minister, and my mom came from an upper-class family; both are from Puerto Rico. My dad earned his master's degree and retired as a major in the US Army.

My parents taught me so much, but what I didn't learn was how to speak up for myself. Taking control, which includes your life, success, and beliefs, is empowering. It's important to voice your opinion, but I'm not big on intimidating others to show power. I had two coworkers who didn't get along because one had a big personality that didn't agree with the way the other lived her life. When I was offered a mentorship position at work, it was to help our new hires. This helps me show them their potential, answer their questions, and provide guidance, not only as an employee, but as a Hispanic female.

I also feel that being financially independent is empowering.

Dreams: I think you need to set goals to attain your dreams. Secretly I wanted to be a singer, because of Mariah Carey, until my husband told me I couldn't sing. I guess that will just be a fantasy. However, I will use my six-year-old's karaoke machine at any given time.

Career: I didn't think I would be doing what I do now. When I was a kid, I wanted to be a pediatrician, but I'm glad it didn't go that way. I received my master's degree in 2018 and now work in human resources and love what I do. I concentrate on employee relations as my main priority. I bust my ass, but my family still comes first.

Relationship: I've been married for twelve years even though I didn't expect to marry him. He was stable, kind, and all about me. He showed me chivalry was not dead. It may have been that he is twelve years older than I am, but I finally found my best friend.

Things went bad when he retired. He couldn't find himself, and it took a toll on us. I felt as if he didn't trust me or thought I wasn't smart enough to help him. I moved home after I was offered a job, and things got worse. I had an affair. I never saw myself doing something like that because my father did it to my mother, and I knew the pain it caused. I finally ended it and confessed to my husband. He said he had a feeling something was happening because I had changed.

We decided to work things out and get to the bottom of our problems. Resentment and poor communication were against us. Since then, we have worked over the years to rebuild and learn. Now we are closer than ever and have a stronger relationship.

Shag: Jared Leto

Marry: Musiq Soulchild

*Author's Note: She says she would prefer to marry a musician, rather than an actor, because they are so sexy with their lyrics.

Kill: Tom Cruise

Offspring: No answer given.

Sex: No answer given.

Shopping: You know what's funny? I love a good deal!! Love the thrill when I find a good deal at Macy's. I've learned that I want quality, but a great deal. Hell no!! If I had unlimited money, I'd be spending it!

Life moment: I have two. It may be cliché, but one was when my son was born. I'm a type 1 diabetic and had several miscarriages. The delivery was bad, and I had to have an emergency C-section. I saw my son and couldn't say anything. He was the cutest baby, and I had made that! It was life altering because I realized that I would forever have someone who would depend on me. Then my husband, who HATES vomit, held a small dish in his hands because I couldn't keep anything down. My son makes me want to do better, eat better, and drink less to control my diabetes.

The other concerns my dad. It was unexpected. He died of COVID in March 2020. It was a time that I had so much anger, and his death ended up saving me. As devasted as I was, I sought therapy. It later helped me start healing from the embarrassment of my past mistakes.

What would you like the world to know about you? You know, I saw this question when it was sent to me, and

I couldn't think of anything. Now I know that I want to be accepted for who I am. I have pinpointed my mistakes, but I've learned to build from those imperfections. Now I'm better, and I think that's important. Be honest with yourself, and be honest with others. That's what I would tell my son.

Porsha's Beautiful Chaos

Friendship: It used to be a big circle. I was a military child and made a lot of friends. But with every move, I lost one more time. It's easy to make, but hard to feel the heartbreak. Back then, we didn't have social media to keep in touch. As we grew up, I saw the flip-flop of personalities in social circles. It saddens me to not have girlfriends. I seem to connect more with guys. They are up front. Women are just more judgmental, and I've never found that real sincerity in them. I want to have women friends who can be in my wedding and share that with me. Not just be an invited guest.

Empowerment: Besides making us equal, it's making our voices heard. We can be our own bosses; we don't need permission from anyone. We will reach empowerment when men no longer see us as just a pretty face. When they see us as their boss, as someone they can't just walk over, someone to respect for all that we are. No more smooth talking.

Dreams: When I was younger, I dreamed big. I wanted to be president, I wanted to skydive, and my dreams were rejected by my family. When I went to college, I wanted to go into neurology, and they told me that it was too much schooling, that it was not a good choice. They put me down to the point that I'm now pursuing a degree in business.

My other dream is becoming a personal trainer. They seem to be okay with that.

Career: It is what it is. It's not what I wanted, but I wish I hadn't given up on my dream.

Relationship: I'm in a long-term relationship. We've been together for eight years, but I refuse to let him bring me down financially. I want to be stable before we get any further. I'm financially conservative. We will be on our way to moving in together as soon as his savings account can help pay the bills.

Offspring: I'm okay not having kids right now. I am not ready! One day it will happen, and it will be just right.

Sex: Even after eight years, we still see each other as a new couple. We laugh all the time, he gets on my nerves, but we don't see other people.

Shopping: I spend money on obstacle courses. That's my thing. When I was younger, I definitely dressed up. Then I started working at Amazon, so now I'm in rags.

Life Moment: When I was eleven, I was diagnosed with glaucoma. I was on four eye drops a day, and, the day before homecoming, I had to go in for emergency surgery. I was limited to certain activities because of it. I had a total of three surgeries. Even the military turned me away. I missed out on softball tryouts because of these issues. Learning to live with it may have been a challenge, but I still accomplished skydiving.

What would you like the world to know about you? I stopped censoring myself years ago. I used to be a bully in school. Not that kind of bully. I would put the bully in their place and go to the other kid and ask why they allowed themselves to get bullied. I would mess with them, so they developed a thicker skin.

Brooke's Beautiful Chaos

Friendship: I don't go all in. I meet people very easily and can talk to them, but I don't keep up with people. I keep my long-term friends very close and will be there to help. It's the people in my adulthood that I have never been good at keeping up with. I think about them, but life happens; then a year has passed by, and I never reached out.

Empowerment: I grew up in a country in which females had no rights but to bare children. Forget education and a career. Growing up in a culture of masculinity brought certain expectations, none of which were for my own good. I moved to this country at the age of twelve to experience the freedom of being seen as an equal. Being in America, I realized really quickly that I could do what I wanted.

Dreams: So one of my first dreams was to get an education. I received my bachelor's degree to prove my family wrong, after being forced into an arranged marriage at the age of fourteen. By seventeen, I had a child. When I got my master's degree, I did it for myself. I'm a nurse with future plans of being an entrepreneur and becoming very, very rich. My long-term goal is to return to Africa and run for political office.

Career: I like my job, but I feel there is more out there for me. I want to get into some type of public service. I thought by joining the service I would be doing more humanitarian services. It didn't work out that way.

Relationship: I'm married, and we have five kids together. It was good at the beginning, but now I'm contemplating divorce. I love marriage, and family is very important to me. I don't think my husband is ready for our marriage. I'm tired of not having all of his love and of his keeping some of his love in reserve because of prior experiences. I thought, going in, that he would come around, and we would connect. But we had expectations of each other that we were never willing to fulfill or discuss. I don't want a divorce. I pray things come together, and we both get what we want.

Shag: At this point, any hot guy on the street.

Marry: I don't know anyone I would marry.

Kill: I won't kill Jim Carrey, but I won't be watching his movies either.

Offspring: Having kids is the hardest thing. I love them, but sometimes I don't want to go home. I want to be a one hundred percent mom, but it's hard after a sixteen-hour workday. I feel as if I can't be everything to everyone.

Sex: I love sex. I can talk about it all the time. I can have sex every day—another way my husband and I are different. I even wrote papers in school about sex, the body, and how it works. Even though there was an arranged marriage, it happened that I was able to marry the guy I actually wanted to marry, and sex was everything it was supposed to be.

Shopping: I'm very cheap—red-tag diva. I'm very conscious about what I spend my money on and will wait for things to go on sale. Or save to buy what I really want.

Life Moment: I got my heart broken. That was back in 2012, and I had only been with him for six months. Although it was the most painful, it was the best thing that ever happened to me. I learned so much about myself. About life and the possibilities of self-help. I had never known how that journey would make me who I am today. I have more appreciation for what I have.

What would you like the world to know about you? That I love my family, I love my faith, and I'm going somewhere. So while you see me running around the world, conquering my dreams, the most important thing is, and always will be, my family.

Zena's Beautiful Chaos

Friendship: I have a small inner circle of a couple of people who are really trusted. Then I have acquaintances with whom I can just hang out. I'm more of a die-hard. If you are in with me, then you are always in with me. Unless you really fuck up. My tribe have lives to live, and they are the ones I work hard to take time out for.

Empowerment: You know that song "Anything You Can Do (I Can Do Better)"? I think anyone should get a shot. Man, woman, alien—everyone should have a chance. I don't believe allowances should be given. I hate that female empowerment has to have laws to make women something, rather than achieving things on your own merit. We don't empower just because, but rather because we are told to, and that's not right. Women cannot be empowering if they are tearing others down. Feminism is not about being equal, but about reaching individual achievement and supporting those differences.

Dreams: If I think about the dreams I had as a kid, I wanted to be a teacher…and I am. Not in a school, but for my kids. I wanted to be a mom, even when I was told I couldn't. Now I am. In that aspect, I have accomplished my dreams. I have more to work towards. I want to be a social worker. I don't know if that's a pipe dream, but I can try.

Career: If you are on the outside looking in, you may wonder why I chose to be a homeschooling mom instead of having a career. But I'm doing what I want to do—raising my kids and seeing them grow into the people they will be. That's fulfilling to me, although sometimes I wonder if there could have been more. For my family, this works for us.

Relationship: It's been a hard one. It's had more downs than ups, but it's made us so much stronger. We can share the same sense of humor without saying a word. He is the closest person in the world to me. We didn't have it easy—my husband being at war, newly married to someone with whom I couldn't spend time, and his struggles with the scars of PTSD from war. Then I had postpartum, and we just about broke in our first year. We didn't understand each other until we got to where we are now. He and I have found an understanding to help each other in our most vulnerable moments.

Shag: Chris Evens

Marry: Ryan Reynolds

Kill: Kanye West

Offspring: Postpartum—I am closed for business. I didn't have easy pregnancies due to thyroid issues and dehydration. Pregnancy was not a dream or super magical. The end product is pretty cool. They are fiercely independent and strong. My daughter is so physically strong, and my son has the biggest heart. On the other hand, I wonder if I'm going to give them away for Christmas.

Sex: When I first lost my virginity, the guy proposed to me just so I could have sex. I was shy and the good girl. It was horrible, painful, and I did it because it was expected. Then I went through a time that I thoroughly enjoyed it. Now the passion and desire are still there, but the timing is not on our side with two kids.

Shopping: Red-tag diva! I will brag about the deal I just scored. I shop thrift stores, sales, Black Fridays, and it's great. Someone once tried to take the Christmas tree that I got on Black Friday out of my basket, and it was not happening!!

*Author's Note: She likes to be comfortable and put together.

Life Moment: Probably the same that everyone had. When 911 happened, I was on my way to work and just as naive about the world as the rest of us. I heard it on the radio, and the shock killed the rose-colored glasses I had. Despite what I'd thought, it made me see what really was happening in the world.

Finding out I was pregnant was earth-shattering because I didn't think I could carry a child. I went from being twenty-four to being a mom. Kind of young and stupid, but I jumped into something completely unexpected. It was scary and exhilarating. To go through it with the man I did makes it all the better.

Who are you: I am always everybody's "let's call Elle." The reliable one, the one who will fix things. But I'm not. I don't want to be the adult; I don't want to be responsible; I don't want to be everyone's designated driver. I want to be crazy; I want to let go; I want to tell people to "get the fuck away from me!" I can be loving and supportive, but I get tired of being *on* all the time. I can be vulgar and disastrous. Let me be who I am…not just who you need me to be.

Dee Dee's Beautiful Chaos

Friendship: No, I am an extremely loyal and devoted friend, so I selectively choose my friends because I plan to keep them for life. I would think that I am a die-hard friend because I'm eager to show you that you can always count on me. It takes a while for me to trust and accept someone into my close-knit circle. Once you gain my trust, we will have a deep bond and probably be close friends for life.

Empowerment: That women have the ability to be owners of their own actions, to take action, and, ultimately, to lead their own happy and productive lives. Yes, I like to empower on a more intimate level.

Dreams: No, my dream is to someday be able to have a support group for women, either through social media or an organization.

Career: Yup, still working my ass off—lol. I have been blessed with great jobs.

Relationship: So…what happened was that I'm married and living my life fully committed to a great man that is NOT my husband! I cannot find the son of a bitch to divorce him because he is hiding in another country. After all these years, I have learned that a piece of paper is not important, not a necessary component in being committed to the person with whom you're in love.

My celebrity marry would be Pepe Aguilar; I would shag Luis Miguel when he was thirty years old; and I would kill Kim Kardashian.

Offspring: Postpartum. Everything I do, I do for them. There is a significant age difference between kid number two and kid number three. The older ones are out of the house, making a life for themselves, and giving me a granddaughter. I worry about them just as I worry about the youngest. Although they are grown, I still live for them, as I did when they were young. I call them, include them, and would drop anything in a second for them. The three of them are my life.

Sex: Let's play! I've thought of sex both ways—it was what it was; it is what it is. I went through my one-night-stand phase, which was far from who I had been. Then I found my man, and the booty calls were great. He answered all of my booty calls. It's great to have a committed man who can play with me in all the right ways!

Shopping: Fashion looks better when you feel good on the inside. With that being said, red tag is how I do it.

Life Moment: The day my grandmother passed away. I was fifteen when my mom got the call. I remember all the adults left us in Texas to go to Mexico for her service. I didn't have a chance to process my feelings for years. She was a big influence in my life. She was my hero, my role model, my everything. She helped my mother raise my siblings and me and always gave us unconditional love.

What would you like the world to know about you? That I am grateful for each and every one of my family members and friends because when I was at my lowest, each and every one of them help me get back on my feet. No matter how big or small the gesture was, I am so grateful for all their support. Because of them, I am in a happy place in my life now.

Scarlett's Beautiful Chaos

Friendship: I've always been emotionally driven in my friendships. I keep my circle small, so I'm a ride-or-die. I keep those I can benefit from, but not in a using way. It's to learn and grow with each other. I also like acquaintances and try not to burn the bridge too fast because you can learn from them as well. Unfortunately, no matter your socioeconomic status, it's not just what you know, but whom you know. My weakness is, if you emotionally scar someone, I will go after you wholeheartedly to make you feel it.

*Author's Note: She takes on a protector's role, wanting to ensure the happiness of those she loves.

Empowerment: For me, it's internal support. If we all work together, we can be in a position of power. As a White woman myself, I am both the oppressor and the oppressed. I have to fight against men to be where I want to be. But minority women have to fight for even more. I live in Texas, where a lot of people speak Spanish, but I don't. That hasn't stopped me from getting a position that I want. However, if someone who speaks Spanish interviews for a job, the type of Spanish they speak can often be held against them. And even if they do get the position, they don't get paid more for it, but end up with twice the caseload. This proves that I may be in an unequal position with a man, but they all the more have to fight for what they have. They have even more to prove, just to get to where I am, and that's when I feel we should work together to abolish that inequality.

Dreams: I had very supportive parents, aside from saying I got my ass spanked. I remember it being a scary and sad thing to go through or watch. Later, I understood that may be why I am okay when others are not. I can empathize with children acting out and the adult getting louder. This also taught me that [with support and discipline] you can always make something out of…[nothing if you try hard enough].

I remember one job I had. The custodian and lunch ladies were just as important as the principal. They provided things that others couldn't. To me, that meant the powers were always equal. I feel if you can dream it, you can do it. Regardless of your job, you are just as important as everyone else.

Big emotions aren't solved with bigger emotions. It doesn't matter what role a person plays in your life; they play a larger role in their own. You can impact someone who will take that to heart. My goal overall is to close the power struggle between people. Whatever you bring to the table is valuable.

My real-life dream would to be open a coffee shop just for teens. I want to start a LGBTQ+ blog, but I'm afraid to be ridiculed, as I am straight. I just want to give our youth a safe place where they can share their experiences and be fully accepted. I want to open an age-out foster-care center too.

Lastly, I want to start a blog or podcast called *Unzip Your Lips*. This is where you would anonymously submit a secret that is eating you alive. Then I would give you my thoughts as to whether or not it should be eating you alive.

Career: I think, growing up, I didn't know. I'm a first-generation college student. I grew up thinking I could be a firefighter, nurse, etc. I went to college and got my degree in psychology. What I didn't know is that I needed a master's degree to do anything with it. Those in these positions never leave, making it difficult to reach the career goals I wanted.

I was a product of fast-food workers. By that I mean that my family thought you were a success if you became a police officer. They didn't know there was such a thing as a sonographer or how much money you could make. Career choices were limited in their minds because they were a product of their environments as well. It was later that I found out there were more fish in the pond than I was told. I am happy where I am. I work for a nonprofit, and they really value a work-life balance. I fell into what I really enjoy.

Relationship: I am a serial monogamist. I have only had long relationships since high school (about three years each). When I met my husband, I thought he was obnoxious, and he kept asking me out. I also didn't want to date a coworker. I was twenty-one, and then to find out he was nineteen! We have a large group of friends, which caused a conflict between my mother and my husband. She didn't like that we had different schedules, and he would go out, because she thought he would cheat. We moved in together four months into dating. Come to find out, she just didn't want him going out without me. We have different lives than what she lives.

I would describe our relationship as independently dependent. People around me think it's either great or weird that we can be go out with our friends or family without one another. My favorite thing about him is that he's tall (but not tall enough). I love that he is trusting, and we like that we can spill the tea to each other. Even if he's not with me, he won't miss out because I'll tell him everything. He picks up where things get left off. As grand as he is, I hate his code-switching. I also hate that he was in the military. He always came back a different person. Now he works for the railroad, and it happens. He comes back with enough testosterone for a squad of bodybuilders.

Shag: Nicki Minaj

Marry: Ashton Kutcher

Kill: Matthew McConaughey

Offspring: We always knew we wanted children, but didn't know when. People said to just do it, and it would fall into place. Then there was a transitional period, and we waited three years. Our biggest discussion was whether we were going to have a biological child or adopt first. We had our first biological child five months ago during a pandemic, and it took no time at all.

I am not necessarily religious, but I believe in spirituality. I had gone out for a walk, and when I got home, I found a perfect feather. I opened Pinterest, and the first blog was "Feather Meanings." I thought cool and read it. It means new beginnings; changes are coming. The next day, I found another one. That night, I had a dream of being pregnant and saw a little boy bouncing and clapping. That's when I took the test, and it was positive.

Now we are headed in the direction of adoption.

Sex: I am someone who couldn't care less about sex. My husband, not so much. I can live with it or without it; either would be fine with me. We didn't talk about sex growing up, and I was petrified of my parents finding out I had sex. I get my gratification from emotional intimacy. That is satisfying to me. I myself may be that way, but at one time I wanted to be a sex therapist.

Shopping: I am definitely more red tag. Like Macklemore, poppin' tags at Goodwill. Even if I had a billion dollars, I would be mindful of what I bought. I can spend one hundred dollars on stuff for others and be excited about it, but I will put a dress back because I remind myself that I don't need it. Then I have nothing to wear. I will spend all my money on vacations and immersing myself in other cultures. I want to spend money on learning about a new place and its people.

Life Moment: I feel I have lived a lot of little moments that made my path. There are things I think of often. In third grade, there was a little boy who was my friend. I don't know what was happening in his life, but something was off. I remember buying him food at the concession stand when we went to a movie, and he wore the same clothes every day. I never saw him after that and think of him often. I think that's why it's so important to me that we take care of each other.

The second one is remembering when I was twenty-one and intoxicated at the movie theater. I ran into someone who, I believe, had a visible medical condition. I chatted with him for a minute then walked back to my group. As we laughed, I happened to look back at him, and I instantly felt that he must have thought we were laughing at him. It wasn't the case at all, but I couldn't help but feel bad. That has stayed with me to this day because I wouldn't want anyone to be hurt by my words or actions.

The third, and most tragic, was a car accident I had just after college. Someone ran a stop sign, causing me to T-bone their vehicle. He passed away due to the accident. What always pissed me off were those trying to console me by saying God knows why, or it was just meant to be, or that this was a just a lesson. As if my life were worth more than his. The only ones learning a lesson that night were the two of us, and he can't do anything about what he learned.

What would you like the world to know about you? I want people to know that I will always be in your corner. It doesn't matter how bad things are; I'll still be here. Whether you're a stranger or not, we'll find a way to get through this together.

Stacy's Beautiful Chaos

Friendship: For me, friendship is the closest thing to a family. I am very particular on whom I call a friend, based on life experience. There are a lot of factors that make me call you a friend. I am loyal, I am dedicated, and I am very protective of my friends. I obviously can't expect other people to see me the way I see them, but deep inside of me I have higher expectations of what I want from them.

Empowerment: Female empowerment is very important to me as a mother of six. Since I was a little girl, I was taught by my mother to always help other girls and lift them up. There are so many things going on in the world that are not being spoken about as they should. I think women should show emotional, physical, and mental support. Growing up Hispanic has taught me what and what not to teach my daughters because there's always that aunt or grandmother who has something negative to say about you physically or about gender roles. I always took that from my family and transitioned that experience into teaching my children it's not the right thing to do.

Dreams: To me, dreams are equal to goals you can accomplish with time. I don't think there's a dream that is impossible to accomplish. I believe they're sort of a motivation for the future.

Career: Careerwise, when I was little, I wanted to work at anything that had to do with cosmetology, fashion, beauty.

When I became a woman, that changed. The dream I had when I was little had become a hobby. Now, I want to work in behavioral health and give back to my community. I want to help those who are in need and don't have the resources.

Relationship: Relationships are not what I was expecting. I think childhood trauma has a big part in how you grow from a teenager to a woman. Every person I have been with has taught me who I am and with whom I don't want to be. Marriage and husband have been gainful, but challenging for me. It's the first time in my life that I have been faithful and committed to just one person.

Shag: The Rock

Marry: LL Cool J

Kill: R. Kelly

Offspring: Love them, but they drive me nuts. It's like a love-hate relationship. You think you can live without them, but you can't. I love my children. I just hope they become better than I am. They're my fuel. They are the reason I wake up every morning. After I had my first child, I found my purpose in life. I can fail in my marriage, I can fail in my friendships, but I can never fail my kids.

Shopping: I love shopping, and I love name brands, but I don't think they are always worth the money. I also make the most of the money I have. It's not as if my dream is to have a Gucci bag. To me, it would be to have a good car or a good phone. Something I can use long term.

Life Moment: I would say when I learned that my children were being sexually abused. Although I had been through similar situations, I knew I was strong enough to survive all the trauma, if that's even possible. But when I learned it happened to my kids, it changed me forever. I thought I knew how to read people. I thought that as a survivor, I could look at someone in the eye and tell they were a creep. Being blindsided by a family member changed how I felt about family in general.

What would you like the world to know about you? That I always meant well. That there's a reason why I am the way I am. That I am just trying to protect those I love. That I'm broken too, but that doesn't mean that I gave up. That I never will.

Jessie Wheaton's Beautiful Chaos

Friendship: It's rare for me to feel comfortable enough around people to consider them friends, although I feel a strong connection to humankind in general. Most people wouldn't know that about me because a lot of people have considered me a close and trusted friend. I've learned how to be that person for others, but I usually don't feel the same way about them. Even in a room full of people, I usually feel quite alone. Now I sound like a serial killer in the making! Ha! I've spent most of my life risking my own happiness and safety for the sake of other people, so does that make me a die-hard friend? I don't know. I usually cringe when someone asks to spend time with me because it drains my energy. If they knew that, would they still consider me a die-hard friend? I don't know.

I think a part of me was born this way, and a part of me learned that usually when I open up to people, it doesn't go so well. I probably won't fully understand until this life is finished, but I still try to learn and try to be a friend.

Empowerment: Female empowerment for me is just validating and celebrating one of the two components that make up our soul. I try to honor both the masculine and feminine part of me and have had times of shaming myself for one or the other. I've made it through some tough struggles as a woman—working through emotional traumas, body dysmorphia and an eating disorder, sexual abuse, gay and straight relationships, self-harm, addiction, and downright confusion about who I am. It's given me inspiration, at times, to connect with other women who struggle with these things.

Recently I discovered I had been shutting out my own womanhood for a while, and I missed it! So I began a journey to get reacquainted with my femininity, and have noticed myself secretly trying to take other women on that healing journey with me. I would like women to build each other up, whether they're house moms, lawyers, trying to make it living on the streets, old, young, gay, straight, troubled, or happy-go-lucky. I'd like the same thing for men.

Dreams: I haven't come close to accomplishing all my dreams. So far, it seems as if some major event pulls away my attention just as I get close to achieving a big goal. I'm in the process of trying to figure out if it's just the result of divine guidance steering me in another direction, just the natural laws of the universe at work, or if I am sabotaging my own success. Maybe all three. My goals and dreams have changed so many times over the course of thirty years that I'm not even sure what they are anymore.

When I was young, one of my goals was to make so much money that I'd never need anyone for anything. At some point, my focus shifted to being happy with very simple life pleasures. Now, I'm trying to find a balance between the two. I've had goals of being the prettiest, skinniest girl around— that eventually forced me to reconfigure some life beliefs and goals. Some of my goals were really insecurities rearing their heads, some have been very realistic and healthy, but produced no happiness or ended tragically, and some were altogether unrealistic. I've wanted to save the Earth, blow up the Earth, perfect raw veganism, quit drinking and smoking, be the next top woman triathlete in the US, become a tattoo artist, and be an exotic dancer, psychologist, model, forensic scientist, mother, and perfect human being.

I'm currently trying to find realistic goals that may actually lead to happiness. I don't know if it's possible to do that and please others at the same time, and that tends to throw a wrench in my plans sometimes. My only goal at the moment is to find happiness and peace. That was always the main goal underlying it all anyway. If I ever figure it out, I suppose my next goal could be to share that with anyone else trying like hell to find it and coming up short. I think part of what's holding me back is that I'm aware of the fact that most of my deepest dreams are more like fantasies, and I'd most likely be ridiculed for them—or worse, they're not attainable. I don't really share those ones with people!

Career: When I was a kid and an adult asked what I'd like to do when I grew up, my best answer was, "I want to be a princess." Clearly, little me was in for a rude awakening!

As a preteen, I was only interested in artistic careers, but it didn't seem practical to me at the time. As I got older, I let go of the ideas that supported my natural talents and began to focus only on becoming something that the world deemed useful and praiseworthy. Something that could make me a lot of money and free me from having to rely on others.

I attended two different colleges after high school—once undeclared but considering a psychology major, and once majoring in nutrition and dietetics. I took breaks between schools to figure out what on earth I really wanted and what the fuck was wrong with me. These breaks gave me space and time to explore my options, have a few mental breakdowns, and question whether or not I needed to go to school to achieve my dream job.

I'm not living my dream job, but I am living out a component of it. I'm currently cleaning houses with my wife to make a living, which is nothing that I went to school for and not at all what I imagined. At some point, I realized I'd be happiest owning my own business, and I do. I'm just getting tired of scrubbing toilets and having no time or energy to have a personal life I can enjoy.

Some days, I think I'd enjoy just taking off and joining the damn circus, or being a pole dancer just for the hell of it. Then I realize that's just one-half of the Gemini in me talking. The other half fantasizes about being a stay-at-home house mom and making little candles and trinkets to sell on some online platform. Either way, I'd have to sacrifice parts of my current life. So I'm a house cleaner who spends all day daydreaming and sweating instead. Maybe I'll hire some employees to make time for art projects, writing, and pole-dancing classes on the side. Maybe balance and compromise is the answer.

Relationship: My wife and I have been married for about five years and together for seven years. We love each other, and I also get the sense we both want to kill the opposing team. It feels like some sort of good-versus-evil battle-to-the-death type of video game at times. That might only make sense in my own head. It was rough from the start, but with long periods of awesomeness for the first four years, and then those periods began getting shorter.

Ever since my near-death experience two years ago, things have felt hard for both of us. We didn't have much support from others during that experience; we've lost four pets since then and a few friends. We wonder at times if we're hurting each other by staying together, or if we're just letting love win against all odds. We've gone through a lot together, and it could be normal to struggle through it. I still don't know and may never.

I wonder sometimes if love is the only thing that makes me stupid. Maybe it is, and life is a series of choices—none of them right or wrong. I can choose love and stupidity, and be happy about that choice, or I can choose self and a wiser life path… Maybe I'll find out that love isn't stupid and that there's some pot of gold at the end of the path. Or maybe I'll find out love is stupid, but there's still a pot of gold waiting for us stupid lovers. Worst case scenario would be love is stupid and no pot of gold.

Shag, marry, kill. So, having said all of that, if I weren't married, and it were legal to kill people…I might shag Marilyn Manson just out of curiosity and need for a thrill. It would depend on the kind of day I was having. Maybe on a different day, Michelle Rodriguez and James Franco. Maybe all at the same time? Or maybe swap out James Franco for The Rock. That would be interesting. See, I'm already learning things about myself!

I wouldn't marry anyone, no matter how rich, famous, and beautiful.

If I had to kill a celebrity, I guess I'd kill Mila Kunis so I could wear her skin and look like her for the rest of this life.

Offspring: I've had this deep-seated need to have a child for ten or eleven years now. I've chosen a lifestyle that makes that longing a bit difficult to fulfill. When I was young, I had a recurring dream for years about having a daughter. She was so tiny or sick that I was always in a panic about losing her. Usually by the end of the dream I did. Every time I woke from that dream, I missed her so badly it was as if she really existed in my life. I've wondered if the baby in the dream is symbolic of my inner child, or if the dream is showing me that I'm avoiding a part of my life that would make me feel whole.

I'm terrified that I wouldn't be able to provide my child with a good life because I still have so much to work through inside of myself. Sometimes I worry that I'm not going to be okay, and it feels selfish to bring a child into the world if I'm unsure of my ability to take care of myself. Finances, emotional stability, and environmental stability are what hold me back.

Around the time of my near-death experience, I had a lot of dreams and visions of having a son. It's made the desire to have a child stronger, and I worry I'm wasting away the years in which having a child is possible.

Sex: Sex has been a love-hate relationship for me. I've had times in which my sex drive was so high I wondered if I needed to lock myself up before half of America knew what my underwear looked like. I've also had times in which the thought of someone else's touch made me want to rip their fucking fingers off. I recently went through both of those phases, and both were very frustrating.

The other thing that fluctuates a lot is the type of sex that sounds fulfilling. Sometimes some good scary, rough sex feels like the right medicine, and other times I'd probably knock someone's ass out if they tried that with me. It depends on what I'm going through spiritually, mentally, and physically. It depends on whom I'm with, how well they can read me, and what their feelings about sex are.

Sometimes my wife and I are on the same page, and sometimes we're not. We've had the opportunity to help each other heal through sex-related issues, and I think that's special. I've certainly got a wild side that's different from her wild side, so we try to find creative ways to make that work. A lot of my issues with sex have been healed, but I think the healing itself has created new issues with which to deal. Oh, life.

Shopping: I couldn't give two shits what brand name this or that is. In fact, almost every time I find myself wandering through the clothing section at Walmart, I say, "You know, even if I were rich, I'd still be walking through Walmart and thrift shops looking for clothes." I have to say, though, if I saw something I really liked and it was expensive, I'd probably buy it! I still wouldn't care what the brand was. If I had an unlimited amount of money, I would search for better quality in some of the things I buy. I wear holes in my shoes faster than anyone I know, so that might be one of those things. If I were to spend more money on things, it would mostly be on better quality food, home stuff, and fun things on which I usually don't allow myself to spend money. I care so little about brands that I wouldn't even know what brand embodies who I am!

Life moment: Time stood still the day my heart stood still. It was terrifying, liberating, beautiful, happy, and sad. Leading up to that day, I watched my body wither away to nothing within two weeks and could feel each organ working overtime to keep me going. I felt a lot of pain and fear, couldn't pee or poop for days at a time, started losing my eyesight, struggled to walk without passing out, and I was losing two to three pounds every day. Eating either led to convulsions or loss of consciousness. I had an unquenchable thirst and was cold and sweaty most of the time. The scariest part was the hallucinations (or visions) and being followed and watched by strangers for weeks.

Before all this began, we had spent the day in the home of a couple with whom we had recently made friends. He was a holistic doctor, and his wife stayed home. I've always resisted traditional medicine and mainstream health care, so we had a lot in common already. We traded services and enjoyed the new connection we had built. That day, we couldn't shake the feeling that something wasn't right, and we both thought the doctor and his wife had slipped something into my smoothie. There had been possible red flags leading up to that moment, but we thought we were overreacting…until I almost died.

The moment I heard my heart stop beating, a big, beautiful tube of bright sparkling, cozy light beamed down from the ceiling of my mother-in-law's house. I wasn't in a hospital because I chose to go to her house for prayer instead.

Because of that, I got to experience what it's like when time doesn't exist. I got to feel how we feel when nothing matters except the love energy with which we were all made. I felt the happiness and freedom in dying, and the weight of the decision to stay on Earth instead. I got to learn that we go on after these bodies die and that true hell is here on Earth, inside our minds, individually and collectively. I got to see hell on Earth in a positive way. I saw that our souls choose to play this game of life in hell because it's a fun way to remember that we are all the same and that we can choose to feel heaven. We're all just playing a role. Everything seemed so meaningless and meaningful, all at once, and I felt as if we were all taking life too seriously.

Once I was over all the fear attached to this event, I couldn't help but love everyone and everything. For a couple of months, I could not see anything as good or bad. Everything was just perfect the way it was. I could understand all kinds of concepts, patterns, and people that I couldn't before.

I saw beautiful colors around living things and colorful orbs of light during this time. My sixth-sense skills were exploding for a couple of months while I physically recovered, and I had the most shocking and amazing experiences with animals.

I chose to stay here, thinking everything would be a breeze after seeing things in this new way. I thought I was supposed to shout the good news from the rooftops. I was wrong. As I got reacquainted with time, my body, and my life, I may have chosen to leave that beautiful feeling behind so that I could stay connected to people in a certain way. I think I was so sad that I couldn't convince anyone of the truth about what I experienced, so I chose to try and forget it. I miss that feeling though.

The good news is that when I finish this life, I'll get to feel it again. Maybe before then. Who knows? It's been impossible for me to forget the day that time stood still, no matter how hard I try. I'm not supposed to forget something like that.

I was blessed to have my wife by my side through that time, especially when I could hardly function and needed someone with whom to share my fear. I was grateful for my dad's assisting in the ways he could and for giving me the space I needed to go through hell. Even if people didn't believe me or understand what I was experiencing, I appreciated them for caring enough to want to help. My real guide through this time was God and all the beings of light and dark that spoke to me during that time. Nature, animals, music, numbers, dreams, and synchronistic events guided me through each phase of the aftermath. The name God does no justice anymore. Whatever guided me through that time was much too big to give a suitable name.

What would you like the world to know about you? I am you, and you are me, and we're all in love with each other. Our souls have chosen to forget who we are, in order to challenge ourselves to remember against all odds. When I'm alone, I pray that we all remember at the same time, even if it's only for ten seconds!

Camila's Beautiful Chaos

Friendship: I would definitely say I'm a girl with many friends. Best friends I can't live without. Close friends who never earn the title of best because either I have trust issues or I simply don't have the mental capacity to give them the same energy. Friends who call me their best friend, but I rudely don't consider them mine. Friends whom I keep around for God knows why because all they do is purposely cause me pain. And longtime friends who make me want to pull my hair out one by one, but I cannot help but love them to death.

I'm one of those people who could make friends with a wall, which is actually quite interesting because, growing up, I was very shy when it came to meeting new people. I was very insecure about my image and how I came off to others. Now I'm just that same insecure person, but with an extroverted personality to hide how I really feel. IT'S GREAT!

I would say I'm definitely a die-hard friend. When you are so lucky that I call you my best friend—yes, this is cocky, confident me—get used to me, sister, because you're not getting rid of me easily. I would take a bullet for my best friend. I would literally strip all my clothes off and jump into a tank of toxic men for my best friend (my two greatest fears—seeing myself naked and toxic men). I'm even a die-hard friend for people who don't deserve it.

I currently have a friend I thought had earned best-friend status. Could I tell you why I thought she did? Literally, have ZERO clue. She definitely put on a good show when I first met her. Acting all sweet and deserving of MY LOVE AND FRIENDSHIP at first. And then—*BAM!*—I find out from our close circle of friends that she talks shit about me to everyone and is also trying to befriend my ex while rubbing it in my face. Have I stopped being friends with her? That would be a BIG, FAT NOPE!

I think I am attracted to those who are broken. Not in a narcissistic way, wanting to manipulate and gaslight them, but in a way that I feel it's my mission to help them through their struggles. I always pick the really pessimistic kind of assholes; my brain is like, *Yeahhhh, that's the one you want to heal; go make friends*. And in the end, sometimes I come out being able to be a kick-ass friend to them, and vice versa, and then other times, I get my ass handed to me TKO style. I think the reason I give too much to friends who don't deserve it is because I have this issue with people not liking me; I want to be liked by everyone.

But I have gotten better over the years. I now realize I'm not going to be everyone's favorite, and THAT'S OKAY! Good Lord, it only took reaching thirty years old to realize this.

Empowerment: Why is it that whenever I hear the words "women's empowerment" or "equality for women," I cringe. Am I a female woman-hater? It's funny because if ANY man were to walk up to me and tell me how difficult his life is, or try to convince me that he is better than women in any category, Lord knows, he better prepare for one of the most degrading verbal battles he's ever faced. But as soon as you label it, I'm all, "Ew, I'm not one of those batshit-crazy feminists." So let me take a moment to actually Google "women's empowerment" and "feminism." Please hold...

Okay, so pretty much I'm technically a feminist who supports women's empowerment, but sometimes I think women abuse those words to get what they want selfishly. Not to go down a political spiral, but this world is going to hell in a handbasket. People have become so entitled. So self-centered. So "I've barely lived twenty years, so y'all owe me everything" vibes. People are also very hypocritical. Some of the women who are parading around shouting for women's equality are also demanding their husbands do all the "manly" duties around the house, such as mow the lawn, clean the cars, and take out the trash. All because she just got a fresh manicure, wants to sit on the couch with a glass of wine in hand, watching the new season of *The Bachelor* while hubby was out all day grinding to be the only source of income.

Listen, I came from a broken family. My mother raised my sister and me while going to nursing school and putting in an absurd amount of hours working two different jobs to make sure her girls were taken care of. I have seen firsthand the beauty that women in general can create for this world and the lack of respect they get. My friends, as well as my mother (when she had me—sorry, mom), willingly or not (again, sorry, mom), have given life to humankind without any sort of pain medication. If men were the ones bearing children and giving birth, there would be no human race. The first sign of pain and they would be begging for mercy before it even hit them.

So I am here to support women. Women have and can do great things for this world because of what we see through our eyes, how we experience it, and what we will put forth to better others. Not to mention we are fucking badass when it comes to putting our minds to something we want to accomplish, regardless of how much adversity we face on a daily basis. But I do believe that there are some things that men can naturally do better than women. And vice versa! Whoops! I've had too many glasses of wine to go down that rabbit hole!

Dreams: Have I accomplished all my dreams? Man, that sure is a loaded question. What are dreams really? Are they intangible things that you will never in your life accomplish if you're being honest with yourself? Are they things you deem important, but then somewhere down the line you realize is irrelevant to your happiness? Or maybe it's a dream that you have longed for your entire life, and you've been slowly working towards it, seeing little progress, but not reaching that dream as quickly as you intended.

Childhood trauma may have caused me to think so negatively about dreams coming true. As a kid, I had a lot of dreams. The ones that I can remember include being a professional softball player, falling madly in love with a handsome man who treats me as if I'm the only thing that matters in this world, and being financially successful while being the most in shape and mentally content.

Well, for starters, being a professional softball player was not in the cards after my two shoulder surgeries. One of them taking place my freshman year of college when I was supposed to be kicking ass on the softball team for which I was recruited. Not to toot my own horn, but I'm going to toot it real quick. I was quite good at softball. Any sport, really, came naturally to me. Softball had my heart, though. I was never more myself than on the field. I led the high school softball team for most of my varsity career. My coach and

I were best buddies. Younger athletes looked up to me. I was in my element.

But that started to take a slow-moving decline when I had an injury to my right shoulder during my junior year of basketball season, and then soon after an injury to my left shoulder my senior year of softball. I knew it was time to throw in the towel, and that is when it hit me that one of my biggest dreams had come to an end. Sounds silly, right? Something that I thought was so important in high school is something that would have been shot down eventually because there is no such thing as professional softball anymore anyways! Women's empowerment, am I right?

Well, what's even better is I've thought that finding my knight in shining armor would be the key to my happiness!? Some six foot, five inches tall, dark, and handsome man to tell me how wonderful I am, to look at me as he's never looked at another woman before, and to put all the babies in me so I can be his walking copy machine!?

Oh, girlfriend, go take a nap. As much as I would entirely still love that, I've realized through my unfortunate but necessary hard lessons that life is much more than seeking external validation. Most of my life, for as long as I can remember, I've always obsessed over the idea of having a boyfriend, husband, or even just a boy to be obsessed with me. Can someone say daddy issues?! Not that I don't deserve to have something amazing with a man who treats me well and gives me everything I deserve, but I've put so much pressure on myself and my life to find that. Put everything aside that actually matters, like my health and career, just to find it.

You think I sound healed, but let me tell you I only just came to this conclusion about a month ago, and I'm twenty-nine years old. Now, reality is, my dream of becoming financially successful and mentally healthy is something I can, and have in parts, accomplished. Mental health is something with which I've always struggled. I think it's something with which ninety-nine percent of the world struggles. But it takes a certain type of person to look inward and want better for themselves. Even if that means being completely honest and pointing out the parts inside that need some serious work. I've been in and out of therapy. Have had my highs and lows, but I would say I've begun starting the slow climb up to being happy within myself.

When it comes to finances, I definitely do not have it figured out. I'm negative in my business and personal account currently, and Lord knows my savings account hasn't seen the light of day. But, oddly, I'm a very successful business owner. I'm slowly learning how to become a responsible adult and not spend all my money on shopping and Door Dash, even though my bank accounts say differently. It might be a slow process, but I've heard that slow and steady wins the race.

Career: All right, I'm going to put this out there now. I am just as confused now as I was as a little kid. When I was three years old, I told my mom I wanted to be a garbage-truck driver. I'm an esthetician now. Went from grubby, dirty hands, sweat, and slugging around bags of trash, to wanting a clean, put-together, calm environment in which I'm able to look my best and smell my best.

Let me tell you, my mind changed throughout my childhood about as quickly as Texas weather. I wanted to be a chiropractor, physical therapist, softball coach, accountant (I'm awful at math and don't know the first thing about saving money, clearly), and an office manager (whatever that means). Then finally a drunk bartender, which truly was one of my most favorite careers to date, aside from the fact that I gained fifty pounds and couldn't function without at least a bottle of wine.

I was always told growing up that I wasn't smart. That I should just play it safe, take the easier classes, apply to community colleges, try to get a sports scholarship because "there's a chance your grades won't do it for you."

The funny thing is, I'm quite intelligent, but have the mind of a mouse. It bounces around everywhere, and trying to pay attention in class was so difficult for me. Back then, ADD (attention deficit disorder) or any learning diagnosis wasn't talked about. If you did poorly in school, you were just stupid. That's what happened to me. I was labeled stupid. What saved me was I was cute as hell and good at sports.

Having in my mind that I wasn't smart enough definitely made it hard for me to believe I could make it anywhere in life. My bar I set for myself was knee-high, and, honestly, I got comfortable living there. It wasn't until I discovered the beauty industry that I realized I'm actually a different kind of smart than the typical book smart everyone praises. I was top of my class in esthetician school. And, yes, we learned more than just what lipstick color looked good on certain complexions. We learned about physiology and anatomy. About chemicals, how they are formed, and how they react with each other. I excelled because it was something in which I was interested. Not just for the material alone, but because I could relate it to skin care.

Now, combine someone who enjoys making others feel and look their best with someone who is a giver, caretaker, and lover by nature—you've got yourself something quite special. I excel in what I do. I know that I can take any type of person under my wing and make them feel seen, heard, accepted, and important. I can also use my attention to detail and passion for my industry to create something bigger than what has been seen before. And we are underway, my friends.

Relationship: For the first time ever, this girl is single! From the ripe age of thirteen, I've gone from one relationship to the next, with maybe a month or two in between. I'm definitely a relationship-type girl, but the reality is I struggled with self-love, so I depended on others to make me feel happy. Staying single for any longer than a couple of months made me have to face my emotions, really feel the feelings. Learn how to be okay with being alone and enjoy my own company. Heal from the past. And most of all, learn to love myself. YUCK! All of that seemed as if it were way too much for me to handle.

This time around, we are doing it differently. I actually just went through a breakup about three months ago. Around now is when I would usually be finding my next codependency victim. Not this time! I'm actually looking forward to this healing journey. I went from dating the bad boys, the boys who had so much trauma I could focus on their shit instead of my own. The boys whom I wasn't even close to being attracted to, OR the ones who barely showed the bare minimum.

I've dated a woman. That was a ride in its own. Before her, I had gone through a period of "fuck all men," so I decided to try the other team. Come to find out, it doesn't matter the gender. It all has to do with whom I'm choosing.

Word of advice, I would highly advise against choosing someone for all the wrong reasons, and ignoring all the red flags, just to feel loved. It never ends well. Being single has its perks. Such as not having to answer to anyone. Having space to yourself. Being able to have a bed in which to spread-eagle if you'd like. Not having to check someone's location to see why the fuck they haven't answered for twelve hours. Or not having to glare at their pupils to see if they actually did heroin before they came over, after they promised they wouldn't this time. Oh, is that just me?

Okay, moving on. I wouldn't say I'm content with where I'm at right now when it comes to relationship status. This single thing is all so new, and if we are talking about over fifteen years of being in relationships, one after the other, there is definitely going to be quite a bit to unpack. I've definitely had my highs, feeling self-gratified and as if I'd made some good progress. Then I've had some pretty hard lows, feeling as if I'm Kim Kardashian crying in the bathroom mirror and thinking to myself, *No wonder nothing works out for you; you're hideous!* But, of course, that is all a part of the process.

Beginning is already a step in the right direction. I am looking forward to finding myself. Learning how to truly love myself, flaws and all.

Shag, Marry, Kill. Oh my gosh, I love this game. It's hard because there are so many I would choose.

Shag—One hundred percent, Ian Somerhalder. I'm sorry, but did you see the sex appeal in *Vampire Diaries*? I'd let him suck me dry. (I'm talking blood here, you perverts.)

Marry—I'm going to have to go with the Zaddy of all Zaddies—Ryan Reynolds. Blake Lively, you are one lucky lady. If you ever get sick of him, throw him my way…naked.

OMG, WAIT. But I love Jimmy Fallon. Okay, if Blake is going to be selfish and keep Ryan all to herself, I'm going to pick Jimmy. When's the wedding?

Kill—Jonah Hill. Don't ask me why, but that dude really just pisses me off. One of my friends was a driver for celebrities in LA. He had the "pleasure" of driving the gnome around—said he was quite the asshole. So, pretty much, I have excellent intuition. Should listen to it more in other areas of my life?

Offspring: Pregame! If I ever find a husband… Sheesh. You know, what really bothers me, though, is that women are made to believe that once you hit thirty-three or thirty-four, you are considered geriatric, and your chances of issues during pregnancy and childbirth are really high. I haven't quite looked at the statistics of this hypothesis, but I think it's pretty shitty to be putting into our heads. It forces us to have this unwanted internal time line. Forces us to choose a mate quickly, regardless if it's a good fit, just to have babies.

I remember telling myself when I was younger that I wanted to be married, have children and a house by the time I was twenty-seven. I've never been so delusional. I'm a single twenty-nine-year-old, with debt and anxiety, and living in an overly expensive apartment. Seeing all my friends have kids definitely plays a part as well in my rushing into relationships. I've always wanted a family of my own. I love kids. Thinking of being able to care and love for a child who is genetically half of me—wow—what a feeling that would be. I'm not saying it's all rainbows and butterflies. I'm sure, most of the time, if you're a parent, you'd love to drop-kick little Danny through the closed window of a ten-story building when he won't listen for shit. But I think it's also a beautiful thing to bring life into this world and learn how to be selfless through caring, protecting, and providing for your child. One day, we will get there. But for now, a bottle of cabernet sauvignon is calling my name!

Sex: I used to think I had a low libido. With every male whom I dated up until one of my exes, Chad, it felt like a damn chore to have sex. I was so uninterested in getting intimate with my boyfriends that I would actually get quite anxious when they asked me if I wanted to have sex. Because I knew I would have to put on a good show. Moan as if I were actually enjoying being aggressively slapped on the clit by his dick. Clench on to the bedsheets as if his motor-boating my vagina while making horrendous growling noises was really doin' it for me. Tell him convincingly, "I'm going to come!" when I just want to get this shit over with.

Maybe that's a me problem, though. Not being able to communicate that I'm unhappy sexually. Not giving them tips and tricks about what feels good to me so that I can actually enjoy it. The thing is, I think the reason I've never enjoyed sex is because I always wanted guys to think I was desirable. Maybe even easy. Not in the way that I was a whore and would spread my legs for anyone, but in a way that they would be pleased with themselves for having me, and then in turn with me because it didn't take them a lot of work to get me off. Let's be honest, most guys would love to not put a whole lot of effort into sex, to just get their nuts off and call it a day.

I also believe that it's about ninety percent mental for me. If my partner and I have been fighting, or if my partner isn't pulling his weight in the relationship, it's hard for me to put myself in the state of mind of wanting to have sex with him. If I'm unhappy with something he's doing or not doing, it takes a lot for me to mentally get there. I like to be emotionally stimulated.

But then there was Chad. Not only did Chad have an exceptionally large member, but he took direction quite well. I was also very physically attracted to him—a six-foot-five country boy with a Southern accent that would make your panties drop within seconds. I had the highest sex drive I've ever felt when I was with him. He took his time, listened to me and my body. He was a giver and liked to please. So, of course, when I'm with someone sexually who is more of a selfless sexual lover than a selfish one? I'm going to want it more! Too bad he was a narcissist who cheated on me multiple times. It's always a disappointment when the good dick is attached to a demon.

Shopping: I may be the worst clothes shopper to ever exist.

(1) I hate physically shopping at malls. I hate people; I don't want to be around them more than I have to. I also feel as if my clothing Pinterest board is straight fire, but when I try to find like items in the store, I feel the most incompetent.

(2) Taking my clothes off and putting them back on, over and over again, is a little too much effort for me to endure. Especially when everything looks like shit, and the overhead lights in the dressing room are perfectly accentuating my back rolls and upper-thigh cellulite.

So when it comes to shopping, I don't. On the rare occasion I do, it's to get one item, such as a pair of jeans from Old Navy or a cute shirt for a special event, one that I find in the sea of stress at T.J.Maxx. I'm not a big brand-name girl. But as I've gotten older, I've realized most brand-name products are obviously higher quality and going to last longer. But since I break everything I touch, like a child, and wash my clothes as if I'm trying to save on the water bill by throwing everything in together, I probably should stick to my cheap buys.

Life Moment: The moment the world stood still for me is a moment I will never forget. Something I would never have thought, in a million years, that I would accomplish or be able to say. It came after my first full day in my own suite as a solo esthetician. I run my own business, and I worked my ass off to do so. I actually was smart enough to pass school, pass the state exams, start from the bottom by working three jobs just to make ends meet, to be able to open my own suite, to make a name for myself, to build an awesome clientele, and to reap the benefits.

I remember it as if it were yesterday. The last few weeks leading up to that day, I was beyond stressed out. My boss had just found out that I was going to be putting in my two-week notice; she, of course, responded to the news in a very catty and unprofessional manner, more or less telling me to not come back to her business. There I was, completely without a job, on my own, and needing to make moves fast. Thankfully, I was given the hint by multiple previous employees of my old boss that she would handle my quitting in that exact manner. So I had planned ahead and made sure I had all my ducks in a row just in case. Trying to scramble to get everything together sooner than I thought, though, was definitely chaotic.

My first day on my own, I was booked from 9:00 a.m. to 7:00 p.m. Straight through. All my clients were so happy for me, coming into MY room with bright smiles, cheerful attitudes, kind words, and showing the most support I could ever ask for. By the end of the day, I was toast. I didn't even have time to think in between clients. My hair was a wreck, I probably had under-boob sweat, and my room looked as if a tornado had gone through it.

My last client was about to walk out when she turned to me and said, "I knew you could do it, bitch. I told you from day one you have something special, and you could one hundred percent make it on your own. Now look at you! I'm so proud of you." I gave her the biggest hug, and she strutted out saying, "You go, girl!"

I closed the door and looked at my booking site to see how much revenue I had brought in that day. The number I saw brought me to my knees. What I made in a day on my own was just as much as I would have made in a week where I had worked prior. I looked up to the ceiling, took a huge breath in, and as I let out a big sigh, dropped to my knees, and just cried on the floor. I've never in my life been so proud of myself. I did it. I finally did it. I looked around, just saying out loud, "Wow, I DID THIS!" What a humbling, exciting, and thrilling feeling that was.

What would you like the world to know about you? What I would like the world to know is I'm actually not as happy as I put off. All my friends and family would describe me as a happy-go-lucky, bubbly, energetic, outgoing girl. But, in reality, I've learned to put on a hell of a show. I use that personality and my humor to hide how I really feel. I'm not miserable all the time, by any means, but I definitely struggle quite hard with my inner demons. I fight on a daily basis with my anxiety, depression, and low self-worth. It has gotten way better over the years, but I feel as if I have to continue with this persona that I've adopted because that's how I've been most of my life. To the point that if I come into work, go home, or am around family and friends acting calm and not as chatty, they immediately think something is wrong. That can get a bit overwhelming when I just want to be normal, but people think I'm having a bad day if I'm not overexuberant. Guess I kind of did that to myself, though.

Concluding Our Chaos

Does our chaos ever conclude? No. We just learn to manage life. We change the way the tide and weather change the ocean. This book took me five years to complete. What started as a pet project, for a person wanting to learn how to connect to a stranger, turned into so much more. I've gone on two-hour journeys with the women I interviewed. I've gotten pissed and frustrated at the computer that crashed and lost six full interviews—sorry, ladies. I've grown exponentially. My life doesn't look as it did when I started this.

Years of therapy have taught me so many things. Know that not everything is your fault. Self-reflection is a beautiful thing, but don't carry what isn't yours to carry. Being kind to yourself is one of the most important lessons you'll learn. Empowerment isn't just about helping others; it's also being able to say no. Perfection does not exist. Failure is beautiful if you walk away learning something new. Success is measured in many ways—choose your measurement carefully, as your soul will have to contend with it. There are many things we are not entitled to, but you are entitled to being respected the way you respect others.

Feelings aren't real. I know, I thought the same thing—*Bullshit! I know what the fuck I feel.* But as my therapist taught me, feelings are just there to tell you when something is wrong or off. It's our personal responsibility to question those feelings and explore what they are telling us. Those feelings could be a response to trauma, they could be telling you to pay attention to your surroundings or intuition, or those fuckers could just be telling you you're hungry and becoming a cranky bitch.

Life is so many things, and we can't always prevent what is to come. I tell our kids to enjoy each smile and laugh that comes their way. Enjoy the downtime when you feel bored, especially if it comes after a busy time in your life. Learn to listen to others with the intention of understanding them, not just to respond. Ask questions. Keep in mind the difference between actions and REactions. It's easy to fuck that one up, and that keeps you from holding yourself accountable.

Dance on the table, give your partner a lap dance, and sing so loud the neighbors think Adele was invited over. Have sex, make love, fuck, and get to know your own pleasures. Drink the wine, eat the cake, meet the girls for tacos, and go for a run. Have a picnic in your bedroom while locking yourself in and watching TV all day—one of my personal favorites.

Gosh, the list can go on and on. But who fucking cares what I think? I am just a regular woman, doing life with the ones I love the most, and finding each and every pleasure I can find. That doesn't mean it always happens.

The one assurance I can give you about the questions asked in this book is that they will change. I don't see life the way I did when I started this journey. I am much happier. Maybe more self-aware. Maybe more considerate. Maybe I am still struggling every now and then. However, it doesn't change that I am much happier. The past will never change, so I have two choices; I can make the best of it, or I can let it eat me alive. Hell no! I'm that crazy bitch that refuses to give up.

This may be the first thing I complete in life, but I have no regrets thus far. So when you think of your basic life questions, ask yourself the most important things—Is this enough? Am I where I want to be? Am I living life to make myself proud? Would six-year-old me look at me in awe, hoping and dreaming to become me? Is the satisfaction I feel enough, or do I want more? Maybe you don't want more. Maybe you want less…and that is okay too.

I don't know where life will take me, but this is what I know and feel as of March 27, 2023…

Kelley and I are struggling in our friendship. I would love to say it will work out because she's my sister, and I refuse to think something would be too big for us to overcome. But it's not looking good. I love her and her family unconditionally. She will always be part of me. I have empathy for her in many ways, for many reasons. I know my shortcomings, and I know hers. I believe that our biggest problems are communication and ego. I say that with the most love I can because to fix a problem, you must know what the problem is.

As far as I can tell, there are three possible outcomes. The worst one would be to never work things out or ever speak to each other again. Life sucks that way. The best outcome would be to deal with our shit and become stronger for it. Lastly, and possibly the most likely of outcomes, would be that we chat now and again, but things will never be the same, and I would have lost such an important person to me.

Will she ever text me back? I don't know. Will she ever call me? I don't know. Will I answer? Always.

My daddy, there's so much I love about him, but what I love most is the type of Grandpa he is. Every Christmas is spent with Lala and him at their home. It's become our safe place. The place you run to when you want to escape the world. Thank you for being my saving grace when you didn't even know what was going on. I will forever be grateful for sitting in the den, trying to decipher lyrics to Garth Brooks's music or watching you meticulously thread a fishing rod then varnish it. Thank you for letting me ride on the back of your Harley and for toasting waffles for me to entice me to go to school on time. Thank you for all the "Jesus Christ, Mindy-Jos" as I finish telling you the newest way I screwed up while you're trying to figure out how to continue parenting me more than four decades later. Thank you for every hug, every kiss, every dance, and every smile you have ever given me. Thank you for everything. You will forever be my hero.

Lala, you made me see the world in a way I didn't know was possible. I enjoy the knowledge you share. The stories of your family. The love you show our kids. And, of course, thank you for sharing your dad with us. The most important advice you ever gave me was to put my marriage first. You said this to me at a time that I didn't understand it and I didn't like it. Years later, you proved to be right. I love that I have connected to you as a woman and not just as a stepdaughter. We may not always see eye to eye, but I appreciate your honesty. I love you always.

My baby brother, what can I say? You're as close to perfect as a human has ever come. I can't imagine our kids not having you as a tutor, as someone with whom to laugh and make highly inappropriate gay jokes. Your calmness brings peace to my crazy. I love how you don't shy away from a hug or from giving your opinion. I am extraordinarily thankful for how you fight with me. I love your brain and your unwavering ability to tell someone no. Your curiosity and love of learning are telling of your pure heart and adventurous soul. Now I need you to go find a man, and bring me back a niece or nephew!

Mis hijos. Mis amores. Mi vida entera. My reasons for fighting so hard. My reasons for real fear. The purest of love that life will ever offer. Each of you has so much potential and power. Each of you is brilliant, unique, and funny. Each of you has taught me more than I would have ever imagined. This world is better with each of you in it, even when y'all have me swinging *una chancla* or yelling at y'all for the absurdities y'all come up with. Thank you for making our home the place y'all bring extra kids who become our family.

Hannah, I want you to learn that perfection doesn't exist; although you're perfect to me. Samuel, I want you to learn to make time for fun, even if you look like a fool. Michael, I want you to know that not everyone who says hello is your friend, so don't fall for the stupidities. Katherine, I want you to know that kindness should not be confused for weakness, not that anyone would ever take you for a weak person, but it's okay to show kindness.

The world is y'all's. Go get it!

My love, you have given me more reasons to love you than reasons to hurt you, and that makes you the most wonderful man for me. You love me past my crazy, cranky, and tantrums. You owe me another sixty years, so don't bitch out.

To me: You done did good. Even if no one knows your name, you are somebody special, and you are enough. Keep learning which bags are yours to carry and which are not. Just because you screw up, that doesn't make you bad. You aren't a nobody. On the contrary, you changed to change the lives of your children, you gave your husband a new view on life, and you have given to others. But, most importantly, you learned to love yourself.

To you, all of you—the strangers that fill my life—y'all are some types of crazy, and I love it! Live all your dreams, change your world and the world around you, and chase your fears with a shot of tequila. And when in doubt, remember that your life is a…

Beautiful Chaos

Let's Connect

Find out more about Mindy Jo Nino at the following links!

Official Author Email

mindyjo.nino@gmail.com

Facebook Author Page

MJ Nino

Instagram Author Page

@mj_nino_author

Twitter Author Page

@mj_nino_author

Youtube Author Page

@mindyjonino1823

www.ingramcontent.com/pod-product-compliance
Lightning Source LLC
Chambersburg PA
CBHW061253110426
42742CB00012BA/1901